30 SECONDS IN HIS PRESENCE...

will change your life forever!

TERRY MacALMON

NEW GLORY
INTERNATIONAL

30 Seconds in His Presence

© 2018 Terry MacAlmon
Written by Terry MacAlmon

Published by New Glory International
P.O. Box 5304, Frisco, TX 75035
www.newglory.org

To contact us, email: info@newglory.org

Designed by Koechel Peterson & Associates

All rights reserved. No part of this publication may be reproduced, stored in a retrieval system, or transmitted in any means—electronic, mechanical, digital, photocopy, recording, or any other—except for brief quotations in printed reviews, without the prior permission of the publishers.

First printing November 2018

Printed by Amazon

Sing to God! Sing praise to his name!

Exalt the one who rides on the clouds.

The Lord is his name.

Be jubilant
IN HIS PRESENCE

— PSALM 68:4, ISV

DEDICATION

This book is dedicated to
my oldest brother Edward,
who won his race and graduated to Heaven
just before I began this project.

Thanks Ed

for being a great big brother.
I miss you.

CONTENTS

INTRODUCTION 5

CHAPTER 1   When He Comes...*WHOOSH!* 9

CHAPTER 2   It's...the Anointing 19

CHAPTER 3   Knowing God—the Key to His Presence!. 31

CHAPTER 4   Welcome Holy Spirit 43

CHAPTER 5   Before the Rocks Cry Out 57

CHAPTER 6   Religion vs. Relationship 67

CHAPTER 7   Lu's Last Lullaby 77

CHAPTER 8   A Deposit That Remains 89

CHAPTER 9   Can You Hear the Sound of Heaven? 99

CHAPTER 10 Finally 109

INTRODUCTION

I can't live without His presence.

I'm not talking about listening to or singing songs that include lyrics about His presence. I'm not talking about an emotional frenzy that is the result of a beat-driven, full of the flesh "worship" service. I'm not talking about the latest supposed "cutting edge" church experience where talented musicians get together on any given Tuesday night to write a new contemporary Christian "hit" for the following Sunday that somehow goes on to sweep the nation. I'm not even talking about the most beautiful of melodies and lyrics ever written, whatever you may deem that to be in your own musical taste and experience. I'm talking about His presence…the tangible, unmistakable, un-counterfeit-able, healing, soul-changing, manifest presence of God. All of the above things mentioned may contain it but are no guarantee of it in and of themselves. Think of it…the glory of heaven touching earth…the attendance of the Creator of the universe…

This is the essence of life to me.

At the age of sixty-three, after forty plus years of ministry, I am finally writing a book. Sounds worthy, even a tad noble, doesn't it? Trust me, I don't take myself seriously. The more I learn about God, the more I realize how clueless I am about God. That's a big reason why this hasn't happened before now. People have been asking for it for a long time. Through the years various staff members of mine have put in their votes for it. My wife has practically begged for it, as she is convinced it will be a valuable tool for the body of Christ. Truthfully, I consider myself greatly unqualified as an expert on just about anything, including worship. Besides that, I'm very careful when moving forward with ideas like this one. I guess getting ahead of God in the past might be the impetus for dragging my feet in the present. But...when the Lord recently gave me the title for this composition I knew it was time. I have been around a good while now and seen about everything there is to see in the avenues of Christianity and church life around the globe. The Holy Spirit has been my companion since I was an infant. I've lived through the highest of highs and the lowest of lows, both personally and professionally. I know when He's "there" and when He isn't, so to speak. I have had private experiences with Him that would make your hair stand on end. From a corporate perspective, I have "felt" Him while leading people in worship from behind my keyboard in rooms of 18,000 and rooms of 18. I've also felt His absence in both of those types of venues. Numbers are irrelevant.

So, this book is about the most important thing on the planet to me…His presence. I will share many insights and a slew of stories and testimonies, both personal and observatory, in an attempt to bring a better understanding and hopefully an unquenchable thirst for Him as you've never experienced. To the many followers of my worship ministry, particularly over the past twenty years, some of these accounts will be information with which you are already acquainted. Thank you for permitting me to recount these wonderful God moments again. To those who are grabbing this book off of an Internet page or bookstore shelf and being introduced for the first time to who I am and what I do, you will need the foundation of these illustrations to better understand of what I speak. Ideally, if you happen to find the cherished visitation of His presence for even a brief moment while you read, as I have multiple times while typing, a special bonus will have taken place. If nothing else, my prayer is that you will know Him better and want Him more than ever when you close the back cover.

Sing to God! Sing praise to his name!

It's funny...I personally hate to read. I have stacks of books given to me by friends and strangers that gather monthly dust in my office. Some of them are probably masterpieces. But my ability to stay focused and retain has to be among the lowest 5% of all humanity, and even that may be a generous appraisal. Maybe that's another reason I have waited so long to pen my thoughts...who knows. But with that in mind I will do my best to keep things interesting and brief (two things that have been missing in just about every book I've begun but never finished) in order to make a lasting impression long after this project is history in your mind's library. So, let's go together and see where we come out on the other side. I hope it's a fruitful journey for you. More than that, I hope this writing causes you to experience many future "30 seconds" in the life-giving presence of Almighty God ...

Come Holy Spirit!

CHAPTER ONE

When He Comes...
WHOOSH!

It was a typical Sunday morning at First Assembly of God in Lexington, Kentucky...circa 1971. I was all of sixteen years old and had been recently promoted from the piano, a place in which I had found myself sitting on the left side of the small church sanctuary, since the age of eleven, to the organ on the other side. Incidentally, both of those instruments were purchased by my father—a successful businessman and a music enthusiast who played the organ and piano strictly in the key of C. Dad's favorite song was a long-forgotten piece called "Overshadowed," which I think he must have played at least once a week at our piano or organ at home for years and years. He was also a pretty good violinist—I think he could perhaps play that in several keys. My mother, also a music lover, was a pianist in the most narrow sense of the word, as she only played in the key of F and, to my knowledge, could only play one song—the title of which I never did discover. Other than showing you that my family was a bit musical, this is totally useless information in this story, but hey, it's my first book and depending on heaven's rules, Mom and Dad just may get to read this! Thanks for your indulgence.

So, on this "just another Sunday morning," it was time to receive the offering. As the organist, it was my job to fill that slot with some sort of musical ditty while the plates were being passed among the 120 or so who were gathered. My spur of the moment selection of the week was one of my faves, "It Is Well with My Soul." You probably know the song well, depending on your age, and if you're a tad musical yourself, you can most likely figure out the arrangement for the 2-3-minute offertory: Intro, verse, chorus; (key change) verse, final chorus, and we're out. Except not this week. The last chorus was moving along with the expected crescendo and passion of such a great hymn...and then it happened. He came down. Halfway through the chorus, without warning, He came down, or maybe I went up. Anyway...Whoosh!...all over me. Hands shaking, heart pounding, tears flowing. His glory had begun to rain on the nice little teenage organist...His Presence was IN THE HOUSE!!

Hence the theme of this book. The last half of that chorus could not have lasted more than thirty seconds, even with the most dramatic of finishes, while I fought to keep my skinny, sweaty fingers on the narrow keys. When His visitation had finished, I was undone, and for a good while after that. As a benefit I felt like a new person from the top of my head to the soles of my Buster Browns. Why? Because for a brief moment I had come into the perfect place of His presence. For that short span of time the "hole in the soul" was filled to overflowing. You must know what I mean. It's what I think the Garden of Eden must have felt like and what the earth was originally designed for, and for that matter, what will be realized again in the sweet by-and-by. His presence, His glorious glory.

It's a gift like no other. And it's the #1 reason I do what I do around the world...lead people in worship. It's all about His presence, folks. Even thirty seconds spent there can make everything new. What an amazing God!! As a sidebar, a handful of years ago I finally recorded "It is Well" as an instrumental with a full orchestra on my Timeless Praise CD. It was and still is one of my favorite all-time arrangements inspired by the Holy Spirit. I love playing that song!

In the story I just shared, as well as the many others you will read in the pages that follow, please do not think me "stuck on myself" when talking about unusual things that I have experienced in my youth or as an adult. Everything I share will be an attempt to give you a better knowledge of the Holy Spirit's involvement in our lives and His touch that is connected with each story. It's basically the best source I have to draw from...personal experience. I hope you sense my heart in every case. I receive accolades from adoring people all over the world every time I minister. I'm not seeking yours here. This book is for you, not me, and to point the accolades toward the only One who is worthy. Onward.

The manifest presence of God is what I yearn for in my personal life as well as every one of my services. It's really all I care about, because if He comes we will have instantly taken a step from a religious exercise to a relational experience. What a difference. I often feel I'm "marking time," as we used to call it in high school marching band. Just moving my feet in place and not going anywhere. That's how I find myself so often these days in my services and concerts. Just sort of going through the motions until He shows up. I prefer that to putting on a show for people and never connecting with the living God. Understand that I'm speaking of a corporate visitation, not an individual one. I am not privy to what God does in any specific person's life in my worship events, which I know happens quite often. I only know what He does in the overall service itself from my apostolic/prophetic office as the overseer of that time together. Many times He shows up...many times He does not. When He does, lives are changed in a variety of ways. Why this happens sometimes and fails to happen at other times is somewhat of a mystery that we will try to uncover in the coming chapters, but really, only God knows. If you have never experienced what I have described thus far, stay tuned and be encouraged; you can...and I believe you will if you want it. It's all about losing yourself in Him. Sounds simple, and it is, once we get ourselves in a proper mental and spiritual place to receive. Let's look deeper into this thought.

Going back to the teenage years we just visited, we had an on-fire youth group of maybe twenty kids in my church. Later that number would double. We were passionate God seekers. As a whole, our church was experiencing a strong spiritual renewal at the onset of the charismatic movement. God's presence was a powerful occurrence that became commonplace in our gatherings, especially on Sunday nights at the end of the service. Being a Pentecostal church, quite a big deal was made about the baptism of the Holy Spirit with the initial evidence of speaking in tongues. Today I'm not convinced that belief (the initial evidence part) is theologically sound, but there was no argument back then. Therefore, it was the one driving goal of every teenager in the youth group to arrive at this plateau of talking in heaven's language. Seemed like most of them had that spiritual notch on their belt. I did not. I remember many Sunday nights lingering at the lacquered blonde wooden altar, sometimes for over an hour after the service was done. It was a regular sight to see young people pouring their hearts out to God begging for more of Him—and for me, begging for this seemingly unattainable gift. This was a bit humbling because I was considered one of the leaders of the gang. After all, I was the organist, choir director, sharpest of dressers, son of the man who drove a Lincoln Continental…the works. I had it all, baby! But I didn't have "the baptism."

In contrast, there was a meek, quiet, shy, somewhat socially backward kid I will call Charlie, who was also seeking this "second blessing," as the old-timers called it. In my great spiritual maturity and impeccable foresight, I knew Charlie never had a prayer…pardon the pun. Of course, you already know what happened next. Charlie, kneeling in close proximity (I think God orchestrated it that way just to get me) began to speak a full and fluent dialect of his newfound spiritual language. It was beautiful. As for me, I still remember my first thought upon hearing this… "What!? Of ALL the NERVE! How could this happen? I am Terry MacAlmon, of the New York MacAlmons who proudly sit on the back row and always appear to have our act together. (Note the word "appear.") I'm at the top of everyone's list! Come on, God…a little respect here, please!"

As it turned out I didn't realize the fullness of the Spirit in this way until I was thirty years old, but that's another story. The point I need to make here is this: Charlie lost himself in the love of Jesus, while I lost myself in pride. There is an abandonment that is needed to realize the full presence of God in any form. When He matters more than me, we're going to get somewhere. Until then, He will wait... and oh is He a patient waiter. My pastor friend Rodney Dukes once preached an unforgettable sermon entitled, "Why is God so slow?" Priceless. You can probably figure out the gist of his message. Our Father is certainly comfortable in the waiting, yet has never been late. Remember, to Him a day is as a thousand years. Time and space are of no concern. His plan is His plan and was His plan from the beginning of time. Some things are better caught than taught. I hope you catch the idea of abandonment, or the (dreaded) idea of dying to self, in order to fully live in Him and accomplish His plan on the earth. It has always been how God rolls. It's well worth the sacrifice, and it is a price that continually has to be paid throughout the walk of every believer. To the degree we pay that sum, will we see the hand of God move on our behalf. Sometimes I've done that very well. Other times not so much. I like the obedient times much more because they offer greater peace and better results.

The "Whoosh!" moment is really what this book is about. I don't mean to cheapen the presence of God by making it some magical, lightning strike phenomenon that hits you and then leaves as quickly as it came. That is certainly not my intention at all. I also would not attempt to make you think this experience is the norm in everyday life, or that your Christian journey is null and void without it. The steady continual plodding of a faith-filled walk is what is necessary to complete this race on which we believers have all chosen to embark. I learned this from one of the first pastors I ever served in ministry, Arvid Kingsriter in Minneapolis, Minnesota. He was a man of prayer and discipline, a true plodder in the best sense of the word. In my time serving under him, we had staff devotions in his office every morning at 8:30. I don't know a church on the planet that does that nowadays. Taught me much as a young man about being consistent with God. That is a big key in running this race. As an interesting note, some forty years later, I have become good friends with Pastor Kingsriter's son Doug, also a consistent soldier not unlike his father. Doug serves on my board at New Glory International. So there is something to be said for maturity in an even-keeled life with God. I wish more of the charismatic world would grasp that concept. That being said, the sweeping down of His glory can do so much in so little time—even thirty seconds—that I am committed to getting people to a place where they can receive this life-giving benefit that puts them in perfect harmony with their Creator. Oh, if every one of God's children could experience this, what a different people we would be. Religion is not nearly as fun as relationship. Going to church pales in comparison with being the church.

I have a great concern with today's Christian youth. It often feels like we are seeing an entire generation of kids who have no idea what the manifest presence of God is all about. I'm not saying this is the case across the board, but I am saying it is where the vast majority of the younger generation is stuck these days. Too many have never stood and wept in a worship service from the overwhelming presence of Jehovah. Today's music isn't even structured to allow that to happen. There are several reasons for this, but the bottom line is, where are we going, and what will become of the spiritual climate in our land if the glory of God continues to grow dimmer, decade by decade, until we are a totally powerless entity? You better know this is the plan of the enemy. Satan loves religion, but he is terribly threatened by relationship. He has a blueprint for destroying the power of the cross, just as God has a blueprint for exalting the work of His Son. Therein the battle lies. If our enemy can systematically lull the church to sleep over a span of time, he will be able to run footloose and fancy free over all we call good. It's surely already happening. In America we are seeing the results of a powerless church. Morality is caving in to social and political pressure to create your own truth. Things that were always wrong are now considered right, and vice versa. This is because the body of Christ is losing its power. Sad but true. As the church goes, so goes the nation. And to a great measure, the church is not going...it's sitting still, or worse yet, retreating. Our voice is not what it once was, and we're paying a great price. God said, "If MY people..."—He never said all people, other people, bad people, or Satan's people. He said MY people. If just His own children will get our act together, He will heal our entire land. How much plainer can He make it? Truthfully, we're becoming a prayerless, powerless group. Oh, we talk a good game, but we don't walk the same. If we did you would see a much holier nation than we're living in. The world is watching, waiting, and even though they don't know it, they are desperate for our leadership.

Friends, we have a calling. He has chosen you and me to be on this planet for such a time as this. He has incredible gifts of His glory to pour out on people if we will tap into it. He has a Whoosh! moment for any and all who will cry out to Him in worship. I'm more convinced of this than ever before. Thirty seconds...just thirty seconds with the King of glory, the Lion of the tribe of Judah, the Beginning and the End, the Author of love, and you will never,

ever be the same again.

As I bring this first chapter to a close, my mind is going to 2 Chronicles, where the cloud of His presence filled the temple so strongly that the priests could not stand to minister. I had a similar (microcosm) experience the night God set me apart for full-time service in music ministry and will share that in a later chapter. But what we need to realize is when the singers, dancers, musicians, and priests all came into one accord... most likely laying down their personal agendas, losing themselves in Him, if you will, saying, "He is good, for His love endures forever'" that's when the Whoosh! moment happened during the dedication of the temple. After that, nothing else mattered. The note I received from the Philippines many years ago said this: "Dear Mr. Terry, we put on your CD for Monday night prayer at our church. God knock us down. We lay on floor for four days." Selah. Folks, when He comes like this, everything changes and nothing else matters. So, our prayer needs to be, "Come, Lord, and keep coming until we are changed from the inside out." He is waiting on us to wait on Him. If He makes himself known, even for thirty seconds, or four days, all will be right with the world and with our souls.

you will never be the same again!

He floods our soul with praise

The ancient of all days exalted King

His power fills our song

Brings forth the anthem strong

His greatness sing

All of creation lifts His majesty

All glory now to God above

He is my melody

He is my symphony of love

CHAPTER TWO

It's...the Anointing.

It will happen in that day, that his burden will depart from off your shoulder, and his yoke from off your neck, and the yoke shall be destroyed because of the anointing oil. (Isaiah 10:27, KJV)

As you know by now, I grew up in a full gospel denomination. Today I consider myself a "Careful Charismatic." This self-created label is derived from a myriad of experiences observed and tested over the past half century that have shaped my ideals and brought me to where I am today. Talk to me in another ten or fifteen years, and that position will probably have changed again, maybe more than once. The Christian life is a process. Being an itinerant worship leader for the past two and a half decades, I have probably seen every level of "charismatic expression," or sometimes "charisma-nia," imaginable. Some of it has been spot on with beautiful results that glorify God and change people's lives forever. Some of it has been so far off base I won't even embarrass God or myself by sharing it. But seeing that distasteful extreme has made me a cautious participant in this last third of the twentieth-century full gospel movement. Don't get me wrong—I LOVE the moving of the Spirit, complete with all the gifts Paul instructs us about in 1 Corinthians 12. No, the gifts have not ceased...what a ridiculous, narrow-minded, and uninformed thought. But I just have seen so much abuse of those gifts: self-serving prophecy in the flesh; charlatans who use supposed words of knowledge to fleece sheep out of hard-earned money to support their own lavish lifestyles; manipulation and power of suggestion tagged as gifts of healing and/or God's power; and on and on.

All of that being said, I am a charismatic. I've seen the genuine and I like what I've seen. I'll never forget when my prophetess friend Nita Johnson called me out at the end of a service nearly thirty years ago and prophesied that God had set me apart that day "for the healing of the nations." That is a word I shall cherish forever. She didn't know that it was one of the lowest times of my ministry life, and I had come into that service telling God I really needed to hear from Him. Of course, neither she nor I knew that ten years after that I would begin to record live worship CDs that God would somehow distribute all over the world, and that would in fact...heal nations. Millions of people in places I have never set foot have experienced the refreshing of His presence through the music. So when she spoke those "direct from heaven" words, I felt the arrow of the Sprit hit me square in the heart. I practically fell over and to this day recall the intensity of that moment. Now, in the natural, I had no idea how a piano player in Colorado was going to heal nations. Of course, I can't heal anything. But in the Spirit...she saw something coming that would far surpass my wildest dreams.

So, regarding this Craze-o-matic stuff that turns so many off and lights so many up, we can't throw the baby out with the bath water. As I've heard it said, I much prefer taming a wild horse to raising a dead one. Many churches are devoid of any measure of life whatsoever. This is usually because they either don't understand the Holy Spirit or are simply afraid to let Him be in control. I can see their point, for the reasons I listed. But make no mistake about it—there is NO LIFE outside of the Spirit. I cannot be a part of a dead church; nope, not gonna happen, ever. I have experienced too much life to accept the status quo. Paul assures us in 2 Corinthians 3 that the law brings death, but the Spirit gives life. He also states it another way in Romans 8 by saying the Law of the Spirit of life in Christ Jesus has set us free from the Law of sin and death. I must have LIFE in my walk—don't you feel the same? I want to be in gatherings where the Holy Spirit is given a place of prominence and can change the order of things at the drop of a hat. Without Him at the controls, man quickly sinks into religion and that gets ugly in a hurry. Sometimes I feel sorry for God. He HAS to sit through those dead services! I always say if life is not happening, let's go ahead and pass out the game cards and at least have some fun while we're here. G-42, O-67, BINGO! What do I win, Johnny?

With levity aside, one of the benefits of opening ourselves up to the fullness of God through the Spirit is a term we charismatics and nowadays perhaps many noncharismatics are very familiar, if not comfortable, with...the anointing. It's not something you can touch, although at times it's so thick you could practically cut it with a knife. It's also not something you can achieve, acquire, or purchase. It is what it is...a gift. As far as I can tell God gives it to whom He wills. Some use it for their personal gain and glory, which is a scary thing. Their reward is certainly in their hand.

Why God doesn't strike them down is beyond me, but I'm not God...you've probably gathered that by now. I have enough challenge taking care of TMac, as my friends have long called me, so I will let Him deal with His servants as He pleases. However, I am very careful who I partner with in ministry, as men from around the globe want to use the anointing on my life to benefit their own ministry for selfish purposes. I've been burned more than once, but I've learned over time to look deeper and pray harder about invitations that are with unknown or questionable leaders. My wife, Liz, is very helpful in this arena. I'm finding a safety in paying attention when she feels something is out of whack with somebody. She's not right all the time—nobody is. But if she feels a check, I back off and look doubly hard into a given situation. We need to be vigilant in seeking out Truth in this day and age.

The anointing of God is precious, priceless, and a "must have" in my life and ministry. I'm delving into this because it is the most valuable ingredient in bringing His presence into reality in every situation. So, let's spend a few minutes looking into this mysterious asset called the anointing. We need to know and understand it better than we do.

So, first things first. What is the anointing? Fair question. For years I don't think I could even answer it with any clarity whatsoever, even though it's been a part of my life since I can remember. Only recently have I reduced my many descriptions and attempts while teaching on this to a two-word phrase... "Powered Ability." The anointing gives power. The anointing gives ability. It takes something in the natural and infuses it with the life of the Holy

Spirit. When that life or power touches it, suddenly the natural ability becomes divine. Change happens. Honestly, this "Powered Ability" has been upon my hands, like forever…or at least since the age of three, when I miraculously started playing the piano. Let me share an incident that shows what I mean.

Back in 1991, well before God had done any promoting of my ministry, I pioneered a church in Colorado Springs. I'm sure you heard of it…Grace Worship Center. Our high-water mark during its eighteen months of existence, otherwise known to me as pastoral torture, was forty-three. The church was launched during a time when I was about as wounded as a leader could be. Details not important, but being in that place made the journey that much more exciting! (Forgive my sarcasm.) Perhaps that is the reason we soared to megachurch status so quickly with our forty-three people, and that counted babies. By the way, that forty-three number did not last long. After two families moved away and a few more just sort of disappeared, we settled into cruise control with about fifteen…well, okay, twelve…five of which were my own family. Getting a clearer picture now? It was quite a time. I was the worship leader and the preacher. If my bruised heart did not kill me, the physical and mental exertion just about did. Finally, God spoke to me and told me to "just let it go." Ouch.

With that in mind, I decided I had a better plan, since God seemed short on ideas for success in this case. So after the church ceased being a church, we kept the name and simply evolved into a worship center that met on Tuesday nights so as not to compete with other churches. It started out with a bang too—sixty-five present in the first meeting. WooHoo!! It was awesome! His presence was all around us, with many faces I had not seen before. Great opening night for sure. But, as God is my witness, that number declined every single week—without exception—for the next five months until there were again twelve of us left…five of which were my own family. I was reliving the same living nightmare twice in one year. Please understand that I am not all about the numbers, but a critical mass has to take place in ministry to keep a vision alive. I had no mass, just critics. In reflection, I could tell stories that would make you laugh till you cry with all that went on. Those twenty-two months felt like twenty-two years by the time I pulled the final plug. I won't go into detail in this book. But if I ever turn to stand-up comedy, I've got a surefire opening bit that will bring the house down.

Back to reality. While the church was still a church, on one particular Sunday morning, we had a visitor named Cindy walk in a few minutes late and sit down in one of the many empty $18 Sam's Club chairs that had drained the church's checkbook and my own wallet in the remodeled daycare center-turned sanctuary. Cindy (I did not know this at the time) was a mature, Spirit-filled believer who was a worshiper and worship leader in her own right. Someone had told her of this little ministry. I remember it like it was yesterday. Visitors were rare at Grace, and this pastor remembers ANY Sunday when the crowd of twelve had grown by one… hey, that's an eight percent increase—where's the offering plates— maybe she's a millionaire! By the way, I'm laughing as I type this. Great memories, now that they are old enough to enjoy. Life is funny.

On this particular Sunday morning, I asked another guy in the church to lead worship. Scott was a talented musician with a heart for God. He and his wife had graciously moved to town to join our efforts in building a worship-based church, as he understood my vision and wanted to help any way he could. He became an unofficial assistant to me, for which I was grateful. So, to give myself a break on that Sunday I asked him to lead the first forty-five minutes of the service, which was our normal time allotment for worship. He did just that. I had never had anyone sub for me, so the people were a little apprehensive, perhaps even stoic, for lack of a better term. It didn't go particularly well, but please understand that all we had was a piano...my six-foot baby grand. No drums, no bass guitar, no singers, dancers, tambourine players, nada; a tough task by any standard. Anyway, as he was winding down and the people were still not entering in, God put a little chorus on my heart called "He Is Here." I had learned this wonderful worship song a couple of years before and used it in my personal times with the Lord. So as Scott finished, I felt led to walk over and sit down at the piano and share the chorus before I brought the morning message. I think I had sung maybe two phrases when I suddenly heard someone weeping in the quiet congregation. I looked out of the corner of my eye, trying not to be obvious. It was Cindy! Her shoulders were bouncing up and down as she was literally sobbing in the instant visitation of God's presence. The other fifteen or so people (who were really not passionate worshipers by anyone's definition—one of the funny things about this church) just sort of uncomfortably sat there with a look as if to say, "Hey, visitor, you okay?". Cindy was more than okay. She was having a Whoosh! moment...thirty seconds in His presence...an audience with the King. Just a minute before that it was church as usual. What happened? Only one thing…the anointing. Heaven's "Powered Ability" touched earth and brought with it Life! Cindy was particularly in tune with the Spirit and it was an instant connect. She didn't know me from Adam's cousin, but she knew Him and His touch.

This little story is a perfect picture of the anointing. It BREAKS yokes of bondage. It SETS captives free. It BRINGS instant healing and change. It's the most amazing gift anyone could ask for, and I am beyond lost without it. I cherish it as much as the air I breathe. But one must be open, hungry, and free enough to receive it. Cindy was, and did she ever get dumped on.

The anointing surely makes all the difference in ministry. Two preachers can preach from the same passage of scripture. One without the anointing will bring a nice tidy message resulting in a pleasant religious exercise. The other who is full of the Holy Spirit will deliver life, hope, and healing! I've seen it a thousand times. The anointing is what makes my music come to life. I have lost track of how many people have told me they play my CDs 24/7 in their homes—even when they are not in their homes. It's crazy stuff, but do you get it? It's instant life when you hear it. Listen with your Spirit ears. I'm not talking about the talent of Terry MacAlmon, and I'm not talking about music. Music can't change anything or anyone. Neither can I. Music is music and clay pots are clay pots. It's the powered ability factor. That's what makes big burley truck drivers come up to me after a service and tell me they had to pull their rig over to the side of the road because tears were filling their eyes, so much that they could not see to drive as Live Worship from the World Prayer Center or another CD was soaking their cab. That's what made three elderly ladies drive an hour down from Denver to our weekly Lunch with the Lord service in Colorado Springs and weep in His presence when they had never shed a tear in sixty years as faithful church-involved Lutherans. The anointing…it carries with it the very healing presence of God. King David certainly proved that as he played his harp to calm the evil spirit in Saul. It wasn't the song, it was the anointing. Anointing brings change.

Ask my friend Bill, who lay in a hospital bed in Scottsdale, Arizona. Bill had an inoperable brain tumor and was basically waiting to die. His wife made one request of the medical staff tending to him… "Please don't turn the CD player off." They complied. One night, as the music played, something happened. Bill was caught up in the Lord's presence and suddenly knew Jesus was in the room. Long story short, the next day the doctor took his weekly X-ray to determine the new growth of the cancerous mass invading his head. He came back into the room astonished. "I can't find it," he said with amazement. "It's like you had a bone marrow transplant during the night." Bill exclaimed, "That's it! I felt someone's hands on my head last night. Jesus has healed me!" A few days later Bill walked out of what was to be his death chamber with a clean bill of health. That's POWER! That's the ANOINTING! Friends, I've told this story probably 200 times. I just teared up as I was typing it. I am forever blown away at the love, grace, and power of my God. I am so grateful for His anointing that comes upon this earthen vessel to bring heaven's glory to earth. All praise to Him, for every good and perfect gift comes from above!

Regarding music and the anointing, especially from a corporate perspective, this is what I've found to be the best combination for the greatest experience. It goes like this: an anointed song (born around the throne of God), sung by an anointed singer (a person who understands and flows in the Holy Spirit), received by an anointed congregation (a group of people who are free, open to, and hungry for Him). These three areas—when present at the same time—will accomplish the highest "presence value" possible. Interestingly, you can still find a level of His presence if just one of those things is functioning. But if two are working in harmony, that level will be increased. And when all three are there at the same time, fasten your spiritual seatbelts—we gonna have CHURCH!

Have you experienced His anointing in a church service or Bible study through some vehicle of music or spoken word? Do you have an area of life where you feel His anointing? If not, ask Him for it. As you draw closer to Him and fall deeper in love with Jesus, He may just share this beautiful gift with you. I believe the anointing comes in many different shapes and sizes. One has an anointing to preach or sing. Another may have an anointing to acquire wealth, hopefully for Kingdom purposes. Someone else will have an anointing in the kitchen to prepare unusually delicious meals, while another might have an anointing to make friends out of strangers. I once had a chiropractor buddy who had an anointing on his hands that went well past the framework of cracking backs and adjusting necks. Miraculous change happened when he worked on people. He was amazing, or God was, through him. The list goes on and on. Whatever God has given you an ability and power to do, do it! If you can't put your finger on one thing, seek Him for it. By the same token, if you're a worship leader, teacher, pastor, or whatever that is not anointed, please stop. You're not made for that. How I wish more people would realize this. Why do something in ministry that is not bringing true ministry and change to people? No anointing—no presence. No presence—no power. No power—no change. Let it go and find out what you can do that has His touch on it. He loves to give good gifts to His children. Find your purpose—His presence may just show up all around it…

He really is a good, good Father!

I love Your presence Lord

Your beauty I adore

Your glory You outpour

I love Your presence Lord

How great You are,

how very great You are

Magnificent,

omnipotent my Morning Star

The angels bow to Your majesty

And worship

You the high and holy King

How excellent Your name

in all the earth

Creation joins the heavens

to declare Your worth

I'll sing to You,

give You my highest praise

And I'll proclaim,

how very, very great You are

CHAPTER THREE

Knowing God—the Key to His Presence!

Great is the LORD, and highly to be praised, and His greatness is unsearchable. (Psalm 145:3, NASB)

Someday I hope to be invited to be an adjunct professor at a christian bible school, asked to teach on worship. I would love such an opportunity to shape young people's ideals and impart some of my lifetime of worship and ministry into their heads and hearts. If that dream ever becomes reality, this will be the first class in any given semester. I will write the following five numbers on a blackboard and ask each student to do the same in their notebook. I'm not sure if people even use blackboards OR notebooks anymore, but I still do. Put yourself in the classroom with me as we look at the person of God through a much larger lens than we normally would. Here are the numbers:

4 _____

17,500 _____

162,000 _____

900,000 _____

100,000,000,000_____

Now after asking everyone to take a stab at what any of these numbers represent, I would fill in the blanks, one at a time, in an effort to bring better meaning to David's eighth psalm (Oh Lord, our Lord, how majestic is Your name in all the earth…etc.)

Ready? Here we go. To really wrap your brain around this lesson, I would advise taking one number at a time and truly meditating on just what it means. Each one of these numbers is extraordinary in its definition and meaning.

4—Number of light-years to the closest star in our galaxy. The speed of light is 186,000 miles per second. So, if you could travel at that speed over the course of one year (365 days) you would achieve 1 light-year.

17,500—Speed of the fastest vehicle known to man—the Space Shuttle. This speaks for itself. Consider how fast this is when a commercial jet flies about 580 MPH. Please keep in mind the above number of 4 light-years as we continue.

162,000—The number of years needed to travel to the closest star by Space Shuttle. No lunch or dinner stops, no potty breaks…just you and NASA's best going nonstop to the closest twinkle you can find up there. Better bring a Snickers.

900,000—The number of light-years to the farthest star in our galaxy. This is where the brain starts to overheat (in case yours hasn't already). If it would take you 162,000 years in the shuttle to go only 4 light-years away, how long would it take you to travel 900,000 of those bad boys? How quickly your calculator would run out of digits!

100,000,000,000—The number of known galaxies in the universe. What I gave you above was just OUR galaxy. Experts have now discovered over a hundred billion galaxies. For the record, astronomers believe that number could actually be twice as large once they explore farther into space. A hundred billion, two hundred billion. Do I hear three?

Now class, let's examine Psalm 8:3 for a minute.

When I consider the heavens, the work of your fingers, the moon and the stars, which you have set in place, what is mankind that you are mindful of them, human beings that you care for them? (niv)

Personally, I think David had an unusual appointment with God one night just before he wrote this. I can see the Lord telling the shepherd boy to take his harp out to the field and spend some time with Him. As Dave began to play and worship, perhaps God pulled back the curtain of heaven and showed the minstrel just how big He was and what an indescribable miracle it is that He not only singled out the speck of dust called earth for His holy visitation but singled out the even lesser speck called man, whom He made in His own image, and then chose to know man so well

He even counted the hairs on his head. W H A T ! ? Talk about a one-in-a-billion shot. You can't make this stuff up!

So, I can see David coming back to the tabernacle—fresh out of this experience. As he walks in, he hears the same chant they have been singing for the past three months or three years, whichever. You know the one I'm talking about—it has five notes in the entire song and bores you to tears with four verses and a total lack of a singable melody? Yep, that one. Now if you're reading this and it reminds you of some of today's popular songs, well...ummm... (crickets). ANYWAY...I can see David stopping the show right there, gathering the musicians around and saying something to the effect of, "Okay, guys, listen...we can't do worship like this anymore. I've been with the Creator. It's not like you think...not even close. We've got to give Him a LOT more than this in worship. I want musicians in here twenty-four hours a day, and I don't mean playing the same old stuff. New songs...sing unto the Lord NEW songs. He's worthy...worthy of the very best and highest praise. We cannot give to Him that which costs us nothing, because of who He is and what He's done." David changed the way the church worships, forever. Why? Because David had a heart after God. He had an experience with the presence of the Lord who had groomed him from his youth. When you have that experience, nothing is ever the same again.

With no intention of comparing myself to King David, for whatever unknown reason, I too had that experience as a little child, multiple times. I can only conclude that God visited me to that degree back then so I could take people to higher dimensions of

His glory later in life. One of my personal joys is when a stranger writes to me or comes up at the end of a concert and tells me I taught them how to worship. It's happened more times than I can count. In reality, I'm not sure I taught them anything, but rather presented a vehicle for God to touch their spirit and open up a new level of Himself to them. But the vehicle was there because the relationship had already been happening for a long time before any music had been recorded or concerts presented. I tell you without a doubt—the glory of His presence is the greatest reward in the life of any believer. I simply refuse to live without it.

I showed you how ginormous the King of creation is so you could see what a miracle it is that He knows how many hairs you have on your head. As one evangelist said, not only does He know how many, He knows which hair is #2,347 apart from all the rest of your adorning locks. This has to tell us something. The Father of all that exists is panting for relationship with His children. He wants us to KNOW Him. It's the reason He had kids to start with... to give love away and receive love back. That's why you and I ever had children, if that blessing has been yours as it has been mine. To love and be loved is the greatest joy on earth. We were created to love. And we were meant for fellowship. The most miserable people in life are those who communicate with as few as possible and isolate themselves. We are made for one another, even with all the struggles and challenges that may come with the package of "other people." God the Father feels the same way. He is not so burdened by our humanity that He turns away and makes Himself content by just hanging out with Jesus and the Holy Spirit, although they are great company, I'm sure! But He wants you and me, in all of our imperfection, our self-centeredness, our sin, and all the other adjectives you can think of that embarrassingly and unfortunately describe the human condition. He wants…us.

I've already shared with you the fact that I began to play the piano with a supernatural gift at the age of three. God healed me shortly after birth from cranial stenosis—a premature closing of the soft spot in the head. With things looking grim, my mother stood in the gap and offered my life for His service if He would only touch her baby and heal him. God heard her prayer and I am here today because of it. I jokingly tell people that when He opened the soft spot back up, I think He dropped a little music in at the same time. Knowing God, He may have done exactly that. I do know this—He has been dear to me and with me through the Holy Spirit's presence since that time. My aunt Esther once told me she would walk into my bedroom as a five- and six-year-old and see tears rolling down my cheeks while listening to a Christian record of some type. I was a strange kid. Things like that don't usually happen to five-year-olds. Rarely did friends and even family understand me as a child. Then there were the adolescent organ/piano-playing years in church. I only shared one incident with you in the first chapter…there were several more. He wanted me. He still does. When I haven't wanted Him in the past, He has still wanted me.

Some of you know I went through a dark and difficult season many years ago, at the height of my worship ministry. A moral failure was my sin. Most do not know that I had gone through a similar battle twenty years earlier, and the enemy returned to hit my weakest link again. This time my wounded soul, which I came to realize, through counseling, began all the way back at infancy, along with present-day pressure, pride, and foolishness, really took its toll. The combination resulted in the ending of my marriage and a departure from ministry with no desire to ever pass that way again. It looked like Satan had won a victory. He had not, and he never will in my life, because victory belongs to Jesus—the war has already been won. However, I did take quite a hit that required quite a healing...two years' worth, and some of that healing continues today and will for the rest of time. That's okay. I agree with King David...He restores my soul—present tense.

It was certainly a rough time, though, and one I deeply regret. One night in the depths of despair, ending my life looked like my only viable option. Of course, this was playing right into the enemy's hand. After all, he tried to kill me at birth—why wouldn't he try again? This was what I can only identify as a suicide spirit, sent directly from Hell to my Brentwood, Tennessee, apartment. True hopelessness had engulfed me from every side. I have never experienced such a defeated, desperate, and dire place, and later I wondered if that's what Hell feels like. But God had not left me alone. He cannot do that, ya know. Why? Well, firstly because He promised He would not, and He cannot lie. That is forever settled in my soul and should be in yours too. But beyond that, He wanted me. He had the life of His Son invested in me. He had put a rich anointing on my head to do His work on the earth, and He was not yet finished with me.

Others were quite finished with me. I think today, some ten years after this season of public failure and embarrassment, I have returned to maybe five churches in this nation from the hundreds that invited me when all was well. Besides that, I have retained maybe five percent of the friends I thought I knew. I don't blame any of those churches or people for turning away. Agape love is a concept we humans don't really understand or do well. People are people and sometimes they just cannot deal with things like this. I would no doubt react the same way given the right circumstance.

But the good news is God is bigger than that. In His abundant grace He has given me a new wife. Liz brings love and laughter into me every day. She is a gift to me. Many new friends and church ministries have come along to replace the old ones. The road is a steep one at times, far different from what once was my ministry, but it's still a road that leads to Him. That's God for you. His anger is for a moment—His favor for a LIFETIME! His mercies, new again this morning, are testimony to that. He never gives up on us. He wants you. He wants me. What a heartwarming thought. The One who has thrown a hundred billion galaxies into the universe...wants us. I have no words to adequately describe how wonderful and amazing this truth really is. I can't understand it, but can I rejoice in it. I am His and He is mine. Selah.

So, if you're wondering if you can find favor in God's eyes, stop. It's already there. If you're wondering if you can really sit at His feet or crawl up on His lap in intimate worship, the answer is an emphatic YES! In fact, He's waiting for that to happen anytime...even now. The greatest honor and glory you can ever bring to your heavenly Father is simply to love Him. That's worship. There is a special place in His presence that has been waiting for you...a reserved seat in the holy audience, if you will. He's so big, yet so small to fellowship with us. It's a true-blue miracle. The God of creation loves me, desires me, counts me as one of His favorite kids. I like that. Why do we run from relationship with Him so often? I suspect it's because we still struggle with unconditional love. I think that's because if we were Him, we wouldn't love us!

I asked God a couple of years ago, "How can you love me unconditionally with all I've done that's wrong in Your eyes?" His almost verbal response was quick and sure... "Because I have no remembrance of your past." BOOM!!! That's it! That's Truth! His Word says He has chosen to blot out our past for His own sake. It says He has already loved us with an everlasting love, without reservation. Only He can do that! We get caught up in the shallowness of loving people because of their goodness or their personality or even their appearance. But if and when they cross us—things change in a hurry. God is not like that. His love is perfect, everlasting, and unconditional. He loves us because He loves us...because He loves us! That truth should be all we need for a deeper intimacy and relationship with Him.

Sometimes Liz walks over to my easy chair, removes my laptop, which is practically attached to my lap, and plops right down on top of me for a hug fest. Why? She wants relationship. She wants my full attention, and she gets it...every time. No matter what I've been engrossed in, she knows she's still number one in my heart (and she's so darn cute when she does this I'm helpless to fight it anyway!). That's how we should be with God. Plop right down on His lap in worship. Sing a song you've never sung. He loves that! You will have His undivided attention when you do it. What a blessing to have a Dad like this. Open arms, always has time for us, and desires our company.

This thought reminds me of when my oldest son, Grant, was a baby. I would carry him around and he would talk, nonstop, about anything and everything. My attention span was challenged because of the length and endless variety of Grant's conversations. But when he really wanted to get a point across, he would take his little hand and turn my face directly toward his and say, "'ookit, Daddy, 'ookit." If you cannot translate baby talk, that meant, "Look at me, Daddy, and really listen to what I'm saying." When he did that, I had no choice but to give him my full attention. He was then a happy camper. And, of course, he was not going to let up until I did look at him anyway, so I took the easy road and gave in every time. Parenthood is a progressive learning experience.

Hey, folks, knowing God, not just knowing about God, but truly KNOWING God, will bring His mighty presence quicker than anything. In fact, I challenge you to find His presence outside of relationship. The more time we spend with Him, the more we will know Him. The more we know Him, the more we will be moved by Him. The more we give ourselves away in worship to the Lover of our souls, the more we receive in return from the Giver of love and good gifts. It's a can't-miss kind of thing.

So, to sum this up, my worshiping friends, we must understand and appreciate the awe and wonder of this indescribable, worthy-of-all praise-and-glory, Creator-of-Heaven-and-earth God we serve. But then we must crawl up on His lap and let Him put His Daddy arms around us and squeeze the life right into us. He's very good at that. He made us for Himself. How marvelous, how wonderful, how great is our God!!

As I wander through this journey
that I'm traveling on
There's so many things I cannot understand
But in the midst of my confusion
I can run to Him He will carry me
until I see His plan

(CHORUS)

In my Father's arms there is shelter
In my Father's arms my labors cease
When the storms of life are raging
I will not be afraid
For in my Father's arms there is peace

You heal all my diseases

You give strength to the weak

You fill my soul with Your glory

Your blessing falls on me

CHAPTER FOUR

Welcome Holy Spirit

And when the day of Pentecost was now come, they were all together in one place. And suddenly there came from heaven a sound as of the rushing of a mighty wind, and it filled all the house where they were sitting. And there appeared unto them tongues parting asunder, like as of fire; and it sat upon each one of them. And they were all filled with the Holy Spirit, and began to speak with other tongues, as the Spirit gave them utterance. (Acts 2:1-4, ASV)

This may be my favorite chapter of this book, even though I don't totally know what I will type from here. I guess that brings the title into the forefront as I wait for Him to instruct me on this. It will also probably be the longest chapter of the book, as there is so much I want to say about this subject. I've had a close friend in ministry and everyday life for as long as I can remember. That friend is the Holy Spirit. I will try to make this supernatural Helper more known in the next several pages. But as hard as I may try, it is the Spirit alone who will actually do the revealing...that's just the way things work. Since this book is dedicated to the presence of God, we need to know more about the Carrier of that presence. That's why the third member of the Trinity is so important in this life, yet so many are unaware of the available benefits of truly knowing Him.

First off, let us establish who the Holy Spirit is. To do that we must settle the issue of whether that's referring to a "He" or an "It." I can take care of this rather quickly. Jesus called him "He." 'Nuff said. I think we struggle with the fact that He is not a fire, or a cloud, or a wind, though He shows up that way throughout Scripture. He is a person—a person who has the ability to come in all of those ways and many more. And for the record, He's not the junior member of the Godhead. He was right there with the Father and the Son when they perhaps sang the universe into being. What a trio that must have been! He is also the member of this triumvirate that is sensitive, offend-able, and quenchable. I shudder to think how many times we unknowingly have committed one of these offenses against Him. Religious folk do that with ease. By the way, each of us has a share in that stock…some more than others. James Robison once said, "There's a little Pharisee in all of us." Touché. If you cannot see that in yourself, there's likely a bigger problem within than thou thinketh.

It was a big deal when Jesus told us He had prayed that the Father would send the Holy Spirit to replace Himself. If that had not happened, yikes! We don't even grasp the miraculous blessing of this divine Person being able to be everywhere at once. Heavy thought indeed. So instead of the early days of the Ark of the Covenant being the only place that housed the presence of God, or later the person of Jesus being the presence of God and the connecting point to the Father while He was on the earth, now there was something, someOne much greater, who could bring that cherished presence to everyone, everywhere, at the same time if needed. A much better way to be sure. Of course, He offers much more than the Father's presence; there's healing, deliverance, teaching, comforting, counseling, etc. The list is quite exhaustive. He has been and will always be my best Friend...with me at every turn, through thick and thin. He never condemns me but is faithful to convict me when I sin and is always there to turn me back in the right direction when I am straying off the best path for my life. He truly is my Helper. I need a bunch of help. How 'bout you?

A myriad of thoughts and memories are flooding my mind right now as I recall the Spirit's attendance in my life and the lives of those I have known through the years. Earlier I mentioned the little church in central Kentucky in which I grew up—First Assembly of God. The pastor was Ken Groen. Ken is an elder brother to me, ten years my senior. (I remind him of the ten-year thing every May—his birthday is nine days after mine.) He was my first "boss" in ministry, and I was his first music guy. When he was elected as senior pastor at First Assembly, he was twenty-five years old. I thought that was old back then, since I was a little squirt of fifteen. But Ken had never pastored a church and was a recent graduate of Asbury seminary. I don't think he would mind me saying that although his intelligence and knowledge of the Word were impressive, his sermons in those early days were not exactly gems, even to a teenager. He, like any twenty-five-year-old who is just starting to pastor, had a lot to learn. But here's the great part of this story—Ken had a reverence for the Holy Spirit like few I had ever known at that time. Being that he was musically gifted himself, he was comfortable in leading our weekly "song service" while I backed him at the organ. (We didn't call it worship back then because no one knew what that meant.) We would sing two or three songs out of the maroon-colored Melodies of Praise hymnal, then we would insert one of those new-fangled "scripture choruses" that was making its way from the west coast to all points east. Incidentally, I just recorded one of those old songs, "Thou Art Worthy," on my latest live worship CD, "All the Glory." It's probably my favorite song on the entire project! If you haven't heard it, it's worth the price of the CD. Go get it! (Mini-commercial completed.)

Anyway, I can still see Ken, after we had sung a worshipful chorus and maybe a second one, just...wait. He would take a step back from the pulpit, hands slightly raised, and just wait. It was as if he was making a nonverbal invitation... "Come Holy Spirit." Nowadays most pastors freak out if there's a five-second lull in platform leadership. That's because religion is alive and well, meaning the show must go on, while relationship suffers or is altogether nonexistent. This was not that. As Ken waited and I played the Conn organ ever so softly, a wonderful thing happened, and I'm talking about week after week, after week. Our Friend the Holy Spirit would make His entrance and begin to touch people. You could hear weeping from the front pew to the back. This would continue for twenty to thirty minutes. Most Sundays during this initial season of His welcome, there was no time left to preach. No one seemed to care. God was in our midst in a way we had never experienced before that time, and for many, not since that time. In those early days of Ken's pastoring, there were about a hundred people gathered on a weekly basis. But when this new wind began to blow and the new wine began to flow, things changed in a hurry. This is a church that never had more than 150 at its peak through its first twenty years of existence. Suddenly there were 200, then 250, then 350, and the growth continued. I left to pursue other ministry dreams in the mid-70s, but the church continued to explode, eventually growing to over 1,000 in attendance. This was attributed to one thing alone...the presence of the Holy Spirit. It was a life-changing season that still impacts me to this day. I'm forever grateful for that experience.

You see, when He comes and is acknowledged and given His proper place of authority, GREAT things happen! Why don't more ministers realize this!? He loves to celebrate the Father and the Son. He doesn't even come to celebrate Himself. There is no competition among the Trinity. Reading the book and then watching the movie of Paul Young's work, "The Shack," demonstrated this in a beautiful way. They (the Three in One) all worked in perfect harmony with one another. So the Holy Spirit does not come to be exalted, but to exalt the Son and glorify the Father. How cool is that!?

Lunch with the Lord

Much later in life, I had a second experience with the Holy Spirit that rivaled those wonderful years of my youth. Many of you know about the worship meetings God orchestrated in Colorado Springs for six years, every Wednesday at noon. I affectionately named these gatherings Lunch with the Lord. The Springs had become the new mecca for Christian ministries. They were moving in by the bunches. Over 125 world-wide organizations had converged on this unassuming city at the foot of the Rocky

Mountains. I had spent eight unfruitful years there, including the startup church ministry I wrote about earlier. For me it was a John the Baptist desert experience of eating locusts and honey…and not much honey. Poverty for my family, and nothing I seemed to put my hand to was successful—an overall real fun time. I actually left the city to become a worship leader at a church in northern Wyoming, aka the ends of the earth, at one point. This also proved unsuccessful, prompting me to move back to the Springs a year later. Surely, we would take off in ministry fame and glory this second time around. Nope. More nothingness, more emptying out of any ambition I had left in me. The Midas touch that always seemed guaranteed in my musical ventures had vanished. I didn't know why. Had to be God. (Remind me to speak to Him on the subject of using "alternative humiliating strategies to get the same results" someday.) Then, three years later, I was attending a Passion for Jesus conference in Kansas City. I had gone the year before and had been overwhelmed by what God was doing. This year it didn't feel the same…not much was happening in my spirit.

But the last night, during the worship portion of the service, while I was particularly unengaged and unmoved by what was taking place, God spoke something to me. This is what I heard: "Gather the worshipers—I want to bring an open heaven to your city." I gotta tell you, friends, when I heard that directive from God, I wanted no part of it. I had died so many times in that town over eight years I was afraid to put my hand back to the plow again. God was not moved by that. He would continue to prod me, waking me up in the early morning hours with the thought of a midweek worship hour. He told me to do it at noon, of all times. Talk about a downer of a start time! I couldn't get people out at 7 p.m. on a Tuesday night or 10 a.m. on a Sunday morning. How was THIS going to happen? My secret thoughts were, "Go ahead and dig my grave, Lord, if you're intent on burying me in this city, cuz I'm about dead as it is. This will surely take me over the edge!" I finally could ignore His voice no longer and, not wanting to use someone else's church for such a neutral event, I asked the leadership of the brand-new seven-million-dollar World Prayer Center if I could use their chapel. I was sure they would say no and that would relieve me of the guilt of not trying. They did not say no. A lady named Bobbye Byerly was in charge of this type of request for that facility, and she gave me an immediate YES! Go figure. Just when I thought I was saving myself from yet another bomb, God decides to go through with it. And so it began. Wednesday, November 18, 1998.

Now let me preface this next section of thoughts by saying, sometimes when God gives you a direct word, you need to just do that thing and nothing else. Keep this in mind as we continue.

There were about thirty of us who gathered for that initial meeting. Given my history of failure in this city, I was quite pleased with the turnout. We did nothing to advertise—people just seemed to show up, somehow. I led the worship for about forty-five minutes, and then Bobbye began to lead in prayer for the city. It was a great time. "We'll do this again next week," I told everyone as we dismissed. I was pretty pumped—actually feeling as if I might have found my purpose for ever moving to this barren land eight years earlier. The next Wednesday came and I was all set to go to the next level. Surprisingly we had half the turnout from the previous week. Hmmm...not what I expected. (Enter faintly sad trumpet playing Taps.)

Now, folks, I am not one who is stuck on numbers, but when you have been in a city and watched various attempts of ministry start with a flourish and then dwindle down, it does a psych job on you. Add to that the insecurity of being an artist, and you have a recipe for disaster. But in my defense, Colorado Springs was a tough town. I had even watched other leaders with national recognition struggle to keep new things alive, so I was in good company. When I saw the turnout in week 2, I got that "here we go again" feeling in my stomach that I knew all too well. We worshiped, had prayer for the city, enjoyed a time of communion together, and then closed. "See you next week," I said with all the gusto I could muster. The next week came, and the same fifteen people sauntered in for another session. I thought to myself, "Lord, I can do this in my living room. Do you have to embarrass me in this 400-seat state-of-the-art chapel? Have mercy!" The format was the same—worship, prayer, communion.

At some point during the back half of that meeting, God spoke another one of those "almost audible" words to me. "Why are you praying for the city?" was His admonishment. "Excuse me?" I subconsciously retorted. He asked me again... "WHY are you praying for the city?" Again, I was taken aback. Then He said, "I asked you to gather the worshipers. I am starved for the love song of my bride. I don't want you to ask Me for anything during this hour." I stood behind my keyboard and quietly digested that for the next several minutes. At the end of the meeting, I told everyone what I had heard from on high. They looked at me as if I was from another planet. "You don't want us to pray? You're asking us not to pray? You saved, boy?" That's the sort of the feeling that was coming from their eyes. But it was settled...the next week we would make worship the only topic. As for communion, the Lord led me to have it set up as a self-serve table off to the side, because it is, after all, an act of worship in itself.

The next week rolled around. Now we're into the second week of December when life's schedules seem to change with all the festivities of the season begging for our time. However, there were thirty who showed up for the meeting that day. I felt like revival had broken out! At least we had made it back to our original starting point. If I died now I would have THAT to brag about in heaven! (I hope you understand my warped sense of humor.) We worshiped for an hour, and it was truly a beautiful thing. The Holy Spirit was smiling...feeling welcomed. The hour felt like twenty minutes. The week after that, our attendance doubled. I was the most surprised person in the state. What was going on? I wasn't doing anything different from what I had done for eight laborious years in that city. The week after that thirty more people were added. This was two days before Christmas...at lunchtime. Are you kidding me? The week after, another thirty were added. Things were going off the charts in these meetings. People weeping, the song of the Lord breaking out, relationships being mended, miraculous healings being reported. People who had stopped going to church were coming back into fellowship. The

Holy Spirit was SOARING among us! The meetings continued to grow throughout the new year. There were 200, then 300, then 400, lining the walls. People of every faith imaginable in our town began to plan their Wednesday schedules to include Lunch with the Lord. Eventually word would spread throughout the country and folks would schedule their vacations around a visit to the World Prayer Center on Wednesday. My first Live Worship album was born out of those meetings and started touching people literally around the world; and then a second CD, and a third. What an amazing time...all because we were welcoming the presence of the Holy Spirit.

I could write about this meeting for another several pages. There were "Whoosh!" moments happening by the dozens in people's lives. It was all about His presence. On one particular occasion, there were a group of pastors from New Zealand visiting the World Prayer Center. They were unaware of our Wednesday worship hour and just "happened" into the chapel shortly after we began. Inside of that group of forty ministers were a father and a son. These two men had not spoken to each other in thirty years! As I was told the story later that day, here's what happened: the room was full of the tangible presence of the Lord. The Holy Spirit drew the father and the son to the communion table at the same time, each unbeknownst to the other. Now if this would have happened on any other day, separation would have immediately followed. But not today. With God's holy presence saturating the atmosphere, as soon as Dad's eyes met Son's eyes, tears burst out, a long and very tight hug was automatic, and forgiveness and healing came rushing into two desperate hearts. Hence the title of this book, again—30 Seconds in His Presence—this time it changed thirty years of life! I LOVE stories like this!

My friends, WHEN we are given over to the Lordship of the Holy Spirit, there is no limit to what might happen. Unfortunately, He often has to totally get us out of the way before He can freely move and touch His people. God had to do that in my life. I had been so gifted and anointed that I couldn't see the forest for the trees…or perhaps I couldn't see the trees for Terry. If we want God and His blessing, He will work on us until He has us where He wants us. Shapeable clay…that's the ticket. It's a lifelong lesson. I'm still learning. But the rewards such as I just spoke of are so fulfilling and eternal to boot.

There is an important key to unlock success in God's Kingdom… listening. When I began the ministry at the World Prayer Center, God gave me two specific words. The first and most important was, "Give My worship back to My bride." That was a mouthful that entailed many things. The second was, "Keep your hands off the steering wheel." That was even a bigger mouthful for me to digest. But as I listened to that still, small voice and then kept those two commandments from the Lord, great results followed in ways I could have only fantasized about. It was a true walking out of John the Baptist's declaration, "He must increase but I must decrease." When that verse became reality every Wednesday at the World Prayer Center, He really did exceedingly abundantly above what I could ask or think. I am forever grateful.

Understanding the sensitivity of the Holy Spirit is very important in our lives. Whether you're in ministry or not is of no issue. He is always there beside you and wants you to heed His voice. He will not compete with you for headship. He will simply leave you alone. What a thought. Before I close this chapter, I must recount a night I wish had never happened. It occurred during my first tour of South Africa in 2003. My ministry had become well known (I still don't know how) down there, and our team played to capacity crowds for twelve concerts over two and a half weeks. Exhausting but fulfilling. On one night—I believe it was a Thursday—we were at a church packed with a thousand people—literally every seat occupied. As I walked into the sanctuary with my backup singers, the church's worship team was doing a song to begin the meeting. There was such a precious anointing on their music. I stood there on the front row, caught up in tearful worship.

It was then I heard my old heavenly Friend, sent to earth, whisper, "Just go on up and take the keyboard over and continue in this atmosphere." Gulp. Oh Lord. Really??? Here I was, a guest in a foreign country, in a strange church, with a concert promoter who had a well-thought-out agenda for the service, and He wanted me to just go up there unannounced and take over? Again, "Really, God? No, I mean it. REALLY?" I broke out in a sweat as I stood there. It was agonizing. Knowing what I should do but battling tradition, strange surroundings, and above all, the fear of man every second. Finally, it was make or break time...and I broke. I couldn't do it. The song finished, the promoter took the mic, and I sat down, defeated. That wasn't the worst of it; Holy Spirit had become offended, and He exited my being. I'm not kidding when I say I've never felt so alone in my ministry. You see, He and I go way back, as you have read in earlier chapters. We've been close. He should have only had to whisper His wishes to get my full compliance. That's the way it had always been…but not that night. Nobody but me knew He had left, but I tell you the truth—He was GONE! I limped through forty-five minutes of fruitless noise on the platform. My singers, Shannon and Shauna, had no idea what had happened earlier, but they were well aware of the powerless music going forth. It was bad…awful. Great time for a trap door on the platform, but no such luck. The schedule for the evening was to do a first set, take an intermission, and do a second set. So as we walked off to the green room during "halftime," my regretful heart was dragging, big time. I humbly apologized to the girls for putting them through a hellish first half of the concert, and then explained to them why that had happened. Of course, they forgave me, and we had a good chat about the situation before reentering for Part 2. I can't say I was looking forward to a second go-around. Would you have been?!

Now here's the grace of God for you. The pastor of the church, a former doctor-turned-preacher, came up to introduce me for the next set and said, "I just want Terry and his wife to come up and let us pray for them before we continue." We complied. That pastor proceeded to pray the most loving, compassionate, Spirit-led prayer I think I've ever heard. I stood there and wept. It was then I felt something happen in my spirit. HE WAS BACK!!! His presence filled my being. Remember, His anger is for a moment but His favor for a lifetime. Has that beautiful truth sunk into your soul yet? Well, we had church during that second half. I mean there was an intensity of glory in the house! He more than made up for lost time as He touched people from the front to the back. What a wonderful evening. At the end I called up all who were involved in worship. About thirty-five to forty came forward. I then told them the story of how the Spirit had departed from me earlier in the evening. Their eyes became as big as saucers! They were not expecting that. I wanted them to avoid the same mistake I had foolishly made.

My fellow worshipers, count on this truth from the book of Proverbs: the fear of man brings a snare but he who trusts in the Lord shall be SAFE! We are approaching a time when He is going to count on us to step out and defeat the enemy, fear of man notwithstanding. When we do, great victory will be won. God put you on the planet for such a time as this. You have been CHOSEN to do His bidding. Trust in the Lord, lean not to your own understanding. He is with you!

I pray that as you have read this chapter the Spirit may have enlightened you to areas in your own walk where it's time to take your hand off the wheel and let Him drive. He's an excellent driver, even if the road He chooses is longer than what you had in mind. Or perhaps His Spirit is speaking to you about defeating the fear of man that is crippling your ability to move out in faith. That is one of my greatest challenges in life. God knows all about our strengths and our weaknesses. Let's let Him be the Lord of who we are and all we do. His Kingdom come, His will be done. Amen.

CHAPTER FIVE

Before the Rocks Cry Out

Thou art worthy, O Lord, to receive glory and honour and power: for thou hast created all things, and for thy pleasure they are and were created. (Revelation 4:11 KJV)

Right now as I type this, I am listening to the old song I mentioned in an earlier chapter, "Thou Art Worthy," from our recently released "All the Glory" album recorded at Trinidad Christian Center in Trinidad/Tobago of the West Indies. The people's singing is so moving to me, and the atmosphere for worship is outstanding. It's the way church congregations should sound— which sadly is a far cry from how most of our American churches sound on a typical Sunday morning. This chapter of the book and the song I'm listening to go hand in hand. "...Thou art worthy, O Lord, to receive glory, honor and power [or praise, as the people sang it in Trinidad]; for Thou hast created, hast all things created, Thou hast created all things; and for Thy pleasure, they are created, Thou art worthy O Lord!" My oh my, I wish you were with me that night as the crowd of 1,800 soared with their worship. Goosebumps on my arms even now...big time Holy Ghost chills! The power of anointed music and singing is quite remarkable.

This thing about God's presence belonging on the earth just absolutely consumes me. I am so done with religion, folks. I am so done with church services where everything is neat and in order, tied with a nice bow on the package, timed to the minute if not the second. That's just a major YUK to me at this time of life. Why bother? Understand that I don't judge others who are there, because I was once one of them; and besides that, different strokes for different folks. But when you taste and see that the Lord is good, not in theory or belief alone, but in actual EXPERIENCE, then, as I have already stated, you can't go back to life (or church) as usual. David tasted the life and majesty of God and could not go back to religious worship. Simon Peter looked into the eyes of Jesus as He simply said, "Follow me," and immediately dropped his nets and went. He could not go back to the fishing boat. Same with Matthew, Mark, Luke, and the gang. Paul, while he was still Saul, got knocked off his horse, temporarily blinded by the presence of God. He could not go back to his religious hypocrisy after that day. And on and on with various heroes of the Bible.

We have got to grasp this in a much deeper way. The presence of God is the most important tool in our walk. It is vital to change our world. If you haven't picked up on what I'm trying to say by now, I associate "Presence" with "Life." Denominational churches are largely empty these days because the life of God is nowhere to be found. Many other megachurches that are void of His presence have found substitutes, spiritual smoke, and mirrors, if you will, that have filled the pews. That's not a judgment, that's an observation, because I have sat through countless services in those churches and never experienced "life." I'm not saying this is the case across the board, as there are places where His life is evident, and I thank God for those lighthouses, but they are few and far between. The last days on earth are at hand. We have work to do.

There are stadiums to fill with worshipers. There are evangelistic meetings to present that bring tens of thousands into genuine salvation. There are masses upon masses of sick people who need healing. There are billionaires who need to give their riches to the Kingdom. These things and a hundred more are not going to happen...outside of the supernatural presence of God. The world is so jaded, so hypnotized with glitz, glamour, digital breakthroughs, state-of-the-art engineering marvels...you name it. Without His presence, His anointing, people will never consider Jesus. The passage of scripture referred to in the chapter title really blesses me. I'm so glad it was included in the Bible because it gives us a picture of why we're even here. We are the "designated worshipers" on the planet. It's the premise for everything I do in ministry. It's the "why" of stadium worship. It's the purpose for being created in His image. More on this vital Luke 19:37-40 passage in a minute.

I have had a burden for the past several years to minister to the entertainment industry in Hollywood. Frankly, I don't see when, where, or how that's ever going to happen. But I also didn't see how a piano player in Colorado was going to make music that would heal nations. So much for dealing with "impossible." I ministered in Hollywood one time, many years ago, at a birthday celebration for Harold Bredeson. It would take me a good while to explain the entirety of the evening here, but let me try to draw a quick picture for your mind's eye. First, it seems everybody who was anybody in Hollywood Christian "celebrity" or "sort of Christian celebrity" circles was at this large gathering. For the record, Harold Bredeson was a Lutheran pastor who was very instrumental in introducing the charismatic movement to the west coast in the late 60s.

(I know—a Lutheran, of all people...go figure out our amazing God. And if you're Lutheran please forgive me, but you must agree that your sect of modern Christianity isn't exactly the "pew-shakers" camp of the Kingdom). So, for his eighty-fifth birthday, leaders got together, rented out the Beverly Hilton, and had a huge gala for him. To give you an idea of the night, sitting at my table were Pat Boone, Eric Estrada, Hollywood starlet Teri Copley, and Terry Moore (Howard Hughes' widow). The emcee for the evening was the president of the largest Ford dealer in the nation...and was failing miserably at getting the attention of the thousand or so of us in the audience during the first few acts that were on stage. I felt bad for him and the very talented people who performed for a room full of noise. The place was abuzz with people talking, laughing, milling around—you get the picture. Fellowship seemed to be the order of the evening. Then it was my turn. (*Gulp*)

In the natural, I wanted no part of leading twenty minutes of worship to a large group of people who had better things to do. But...the Spirit of the Lord came upon me. In thirty seconds I had them...all of them. It was miraculous. I had them stand and I hit "You Deserve the Glory" on my IPod, and before you know it God was all over the place. We had a beautiful time together. A couple of years ago I was talking to Aglow president Jane Hanson Hoyt's husband, Tony, who happened to be at that event back in 2003. Tony told me that while I was leading that night, people were being touched all over the room. Some got saved, some healed, some even were falling out under the power of the Spirit. I had no idea…just the piano player here.

You see, this is what I'm talking about. Remember, the anointing brings His presence, which releases His power. Hollywood has the most talented people in the world living among it, but it does not have the Spirit of the living God falling upon it. This is why I believe God is going to open a door in the last days for ministries like mine. The anointing needs to do some heavy yokebreaking in that town. It's going to happen. Write it down. He's going to overwhelm Hollywood with His glory. Whether I'm a part of it or not is unimportant, but I know there's something there waiting for my gift. Timing…timing is everything. The King is going to make Himself known in places you never dreamed possible, in His perfect time. Have I mentioned the earth belongs to God and the fullness thereof?! Get ready for His glory, people. More than that, BE the one He taps to work for Him. Remember, it is no accident you are here now. He saw it before He ever threw this spinning globe into space. Destiny…we have a DESTINY!! It's about time we get healed from our past so it doesn't hinder our present, and is powerless to affect our future.

The authentic is begging to overshadow the counterfeit. Relationship is screaming to be chosen over religion. Years ago, I was ministering on a Sunday morning at a church in western Pennsylvania. I don't even recall the name of the church—it's been a good while. The sanctuary was totally packed that day…maybe 900 in attendance if I had to guess. There was a sweet presence of the

Lord among us, and I decided to just open the altars for anyone who wanted to come and seek Him during worship. At that invitation about forty people slowly made their way to the front for a deeper drink of the Lord. Of course, there's no special blessing for leaving your seat and walking forward, but sometimes that act of faith in itself can unlock something in your heart that brings a greater release. So, I was singing one of my usual intimate love songs to Jesus when I heard a lady to my left start to get a bit more vocal than the rest of the group kneeling at the front. "It's real... it's real," she proclaimed. Then louder, "It's REAL, IT'S REAL!!" Then even louder as the ushers came up to maintain order if needed. "IT'S REALLLLLL!!!!!!!!!!!" she screamed! With that she jumped to her feet and was about to charge the platform to grab me for a relay race around the church or whatever she had in mind. Those around her restrained her. (Whew!) I'm glad there wasn't an outbreak at the keyboard with her and me, but my spirit sensed this was not a bad thing. She was not a lunatic. She was having a "before the rocks cry out" experience...a Whoosh! moment that was too wonderful to contain. This dear woman got saved that day. Oh, she had been saved for a long time in theory and even confession. She knew the lingo, talked the talk, but on this Sunday morning, she met Jesus—not the historical figure we read about in the Bible, she met...HIM. I hope you catch what I'm saying here. After the service I asked one of the pastors if he knew who that lady was. He said, "Oh yes. She used to work on our staff, in the custodial department. At one point she became upset with the church, quit her job, and just disappeared. That was over a year ago. She has not been back until today." I can guarantee you that until that day this woman had served God out of obedience alone. That's a good thing in itself, but at some point, obedience will not carry you through when the going gets tough. You have to go deeper. You have to "meet" Jesus. Again, I'm not talking about church attendance or singing songs or taking notes on a sermon or underlining Bible verses. I'm talking about you and Him, face to face.

Now back to the theme of this chapter. The religious ones around our Lord on that day of praise and palm branches just didn't "get it." That's why He had to look at them and point to a rock. If you ask me, this is proof beyond argument that this planet was made to be the worship center of the universe. I have often said that earthquakes happen because praise is not going forth. The bowels of the earth are regurgitating in rebellion. Worship has been foreordained from the foundations of this planet. It IS going to happen. His glory IS going to cover the earth as the waters cover the seas. This gives us purpose. This gives us priority in ordering our walk. First worship, then everything else. Make it the background of every form of giving you do for others. Think about this for a moment with me. When this week has ended, my schedule will have included the following: Liz and I having dinner with our pastor and his wife; both of us spending several hours with the wife of a good friend who is having open heart surgery; sitting at my grand piano at home playing and singing for my Lord; playing golf with one of my board members on a little course that sits right on Lake Lewisville here in the DFW area; working in my studio tweaking a background track; preparing to minister in a neighboring community on Sunday and then getting ready for next week's trip to Maryland and Ohio for more ministry; Liz and I having dinner with this week's host pastor and his wife after my Saturday soundcheck; power walking three miles at least once, usually two to three times (a personal commitment I made to God after my brother's passing); and working on a couple of chapters for this book. That is a fairly wide scope of activities, and who knows what else will be added to the list when all is said and done. I tell you the truth; there will have been worship released in every one of those situations. Life is what you make it. So, make it worship. You may have heard the phrase, or something like it, that goes, "Everyone worships, it's the object of our worship that is the question." By His grace I will have brought my love for God into each of the above situations. That's worship. Has it consumed me every hour of every day? Heck no, I'm still human. I love sports—especially golf; I love to eat, and I love movies. Not a whole lot of worship going on in those things. A lot of people think I have a cot in the throne room and hang out with Jesus 24/7. I have way more cracks in my clay pot for that to be the case. But we can find adoration of God showing itself in many ways in our daily walk. Fellowship with Him offers great rewards. When we include Him in every situation, every situation gets better.

Now looking at the previously mentioned scripture, let us understand the situation on that day in Jerusalem. Quoting the New Living Translation:

When he (Jesus) reached the place where the road started down the Mount of Olives, all of his followers began to shout and sing as they walked along, praising God for all the wonderful miracles they had seen. "Blessings on the King who comes in the name of the LORD! Peace in heaven, and glory in highest heaven!" But some of the Pharisees among the crowd said, "Teacher, rebuke your followers for saying things like that!" He replied, "If they kept quiet, the stones along the road would burst into cheers!"

Think about what it would take for a stone to cry out unto God. It's a rock. No brain, no soul, no heartbeat, no eyes, arms, hands or legs. It's...a rock. How huge is this statement when you consider the lifeless lump of weight that is a rock? I think Jesus looked around and chose the most insignificant thing He could find to prove His point. He was good at that. He hoped that the Pharisees, along with all His followers, would "get it." On the previously mentioned "All the Glory" CD, while under His anointing and in His presence, I cried out, "This is life indeed, to worship You in spirit and truth. This is life!" That's it, folks. The people of Jerusalem had finally discovered Life. Once they came into the reality that the King of glory was among them, their praise was immediate, passionate, and unquenchable. We must be careful when pointing our finger at those who are way more vocal and dramatic in their worship offering to the Lord than that with which we are comfortable. We may easily find ourselves in some Pharisaical shoes if we do that. I'm sure that's how the people looked to the religious leaders on that day. Food for thought. Somebody once said the definition of a fanatic is somebody who loves Jesus more than you. Think about that for a minute or two.

King David made no apologies for his zeal in worship for his King. He realized early on that worship was life, and everything else was a side bar. Oh, that we would operate the same way. We give God so little time, so little adoration. Yet this entire 70+ years we call life is about Him, not us. He made us...for His glory. He made us...for His pleasure. Before the rocks cry out in my own life, I am going to be a praise initiator. When I worship in our home church as a member of the congregation, everyone knows it. I'm not trying to show off or be a spectacle, I just am having fellowship with my Lord. That's the only way I know how to worship...with all of me. People tell me it brings life into the atmosphere. I am simply giving God my best. Sometimes I am more vocal than other times, depending on song selection and the level of corporate anointing I am sensing on a given day. But we gather to worship as much as anything. Everyone needs to give their best.

One of the great memories of the past is ministering at Jack Hayford's Church on the Way in Van Nuys, California. The people in that fellowship had been taught early on to be vocally active in worship by Pastor Jack. From the front row to the back, when we sang, everyone was singing...everyone, loudly. When it was time to pray, from the front row to the back, everyone prayed...out loud and loudly. I remember saying to myself, "THIS is what the New Testament church should look and sound like around the world." Had I lived within fifty miles of that place, it would have surely been my church home. Ministering there was a privilege and a pleasure. God bless Dr. Hayford for being a pioneer in worship and a mentor to many...myself included. I would like nothing more than to stand before God someday, knowing I have done all I could do for worship on the earth so the rocks would never come close to crying out in my stead. May our lives be full of all kinds of worship to the King. You can do this...you were made for it!

CHAPTER SIX

Religion vs. Relationship

For the law of the Spirit of life in Christ Jesus has set you free from the law of sin and death. (Romans 8:2, NASB)

As the last chapter was my favorite, this may be the most important chapter in the book, for it affects every one of us. I have touched on the topic several times throughout the pages of this book. I will no doubt touch on it again in the upcoming chapters. This is a biggie for me...a spiritual "pet peeve" I guess you could say. That's probably because I see it in a vast majority of Christianity, especially the local church, where I find myself ministering most of the time around the world. I found it again just last week as I was the guest of a really nice church of several hundred whose pastor I call friend. And also, when I take time to do some serious self-examination, I can find it in me, in one area or another. It can creep in when you least expect it. It's quite sickening. It's what Jesus avoided at any cost. I think this is why He liked being around children so much. Pure love there. His avoidance of and disdain for the lofty, pious ones should be a glaring siren to us all, but often goes unnoticed. What am I really talking about? A religious spirit. Now if you are wondering where that phrase is found in the Bible I have no reference for you, but I do have an example that is quite telling in my opinion. Let's look at David and his wife Michal in 2 Samuel 6. As you read this please understand that a religious spirit is rooted in pride, that ugly thing that is at the root of all sin. Here we go:

Vs 16. As the ark of the LORD was entering the City of David, Saul's daughter Michal looked down from a window and saw King David leaping and dancing before the LORD, and despised him in her heart. As soon as David returned home to bless his own household, Michal came out to meet him. "How the king of Israel has distinguished himself today!" she said. "He has uncovered himself today in the sight of the maidservants of his subjects, like a vulgar person would do". But David said to Michal, "I was dancing before the LORD who chose me over your father and all his house when He appointed me ruler over the LORD's people Israel. I will celebrate before the LORD, and I will humiliate and humble myself even more than this. Yet I will be honored by the maidservants of whom you have spoken. And Michal the daughter of Saul had no children to the day of her death. (Berean Study Bible)

Wow. "And Michal had no children to the day of her death." Oh friends, do you see this!? More importantly, can you see yourself in this!? I surely can. What a revealing story of how a prideful spirit of religion can rob us of the will and joy that God has for us. It will try to keep you from spending even thirty seconds in the overwhelmingly satisfying presence of almighty God. It will cause you to judge the way others live or worship. It will rear its ugly head in a pastor's sermon or in the way you perceive that sermon. It will divide churches as quick as anything. The enemy of our soul loves religion. He senses no threat by that whatsoever. This is because religion is void of relationship. It's also because religion is forever in a relentless war with relationship. You can't have both. Once relationship with God comes in its fullness, there's no need to search for God or try to please Him through religion. A set of rules and regulations no longer dictates our every thought and action. When we're free to love our Creator, we become a serious problem for Satan and his minions. Religion kills. Relationship thrills. Let's delve into this a bit.

First of all, Romans, mentioned under the chapter title here, is a fascinating verse. In verse one of that chapter we read that there's no condemnation for any who are in Christ Jesus. The key words that are often overlooked in verse two are #1, "law", and #2, "has." The word "law" obviously is not a physical law of God like one of the Ten Commandments, but an unseen or intangible law that takes place automatically as a benefit of being in Christ. It's something that actually happens when you really do come alive in Him. The law of gravity just happens when you drop a ball off a table and contacts it hits the floor. No predetermination needs to take place on how big the ball is, what color it is, how long it's been a ball, or how high it will bounce once it leaves the surface of the table. It just falls straight to the ground. Gotta love those automatic laws. The "law of the Spirit of life" is also an automatic law when we are truly alive in, and in love with, Jesus. That's where the second word of note, "has," comes in. When you are alive in Jesus, and as soon as you're alive in Jesus, it's a done deal. Not "the Spirit of life will set you free," but "the Spirit of life HAS set you free." Take the gift of freedom and run like the wind. It's yours to enjoy in every area of life. Strangely, sometimes you can be free in one area and bound in the next. I guess that's the complexity of the human spirit. I see it all the time in ministry leaders, and I see it in myself as I've already confessed. Let me stop right here and pose the question: is this law in effect in your life right now? Or are you on autopilot, going through the motions of Christianity without experiencing the spiritual electricity of the freshness of the Holy Spirit's touch? By default, that would be the law of sin and death in operation in your life. If you're stuck in a rut of staleness, this book is not to condemn you—it's to WAKE YOU UP!! There's a lot more out there designed for your life and your passion. Don't settle for the status quo. Settle for Jesus in all of His Glory!

Back in chapter 5 I talked about a lady who came to the altar during worship and met Jesus for the first time. Her life is a prime example and microcosm of what this chapter is all about. She was living lost in the spirit of religion—the law of sin and death. Trying to do the right things, say the right things, probably looking down on those who were in leadership with a critical attitude, and on and on until that spirit drove her right out of the church and any fellowship she might have had with other believers. Then, the Law of the Spirit of Life entered the room on a Sunday morning. She may not have even been looking for that law—it just happened when by the grace of God she was able to encounter the eyes of a living, loving Savior for the first time. Suddenly nothing else mattered...not what people were wearing, not how preachers were preaching or singers were singing, and not how she looked to anyone else...NOTHING!! The Law of the Spirit of Life in Christ Jesus had instantly SET HER FREE from the law of sin and death. Woohoo! This is LIVIN', baby!! Relationship is SO MUCH better than religion.

This brings to remembrance a time when God introduced me to the victory and freedom of praise music. Up to that point, I had never been much of a praiser, just a worshiper. Even though I am known as an intimate worshiper around the world, much of that is because I learned the secret of victorious praise a long time ago. Allow me to expound.

In 1985 I spent a year living and working in a church in Dayton, Ohio. It was a growing, classy, conservative, everything done right, Assemblies of God church. For those who know me and the church I was serving in, my assessment just now is not a critical one, for I thoroughly enjoyed being a part of that work for the year I was there. Great people, some of whom I still call good friends today. This story is not about that ministry at all… it's about what the Lord needed to do in moi. In the spring of that year we as a staff had traveled to one of the annual three-day ministers' functions called "District Council," which happened to be held that year in a church in Cincinnati, about an hour's drive from Dayton. Because the conference was at a host church, the first night's worship was led by the local church's Minister of Music. We didn't call them worship pastors back then. That title evolved as we all became "cooler" in our craft much later. Anyway, the somewhat renegade leader whose name I have long forgotten opened the night with a little chorus that was new to most of us, if not all of us. It had a hand-clapping, toe-tapping beat to it and went like this, in case you're familiar: "The Lord reigneth, the Lord reigneth, blessed be the name of the Lord; for the Lord our God, Omnipotent, reigneth in majesty." That's all there was to the song...a quick little eighteen-second jobbie. We probably sang it four or five times, and if memory serves, there was a key change along the way (one of my favorite musical stimuli that still today gets constant use in my own arrangements). The rest of the worship time took place, and then we went on with the meeting, none of which I have any recollection.

Now mind you, coming into this service, I was not (emphasis on NOT) a fan of those up-tempo, cute little dealios that passed as praise songs. In my professional opinion they were a complete waste of time. Do you know WHYYYYYY????? Because it was just noise—loud noise at that, with clanging cymbals no less, and in my opinion God was too HOLY to appreciate that kind of noise complete with the repetitive phrases and all the rest that went with it. My friends, I, the great anointed worshiper, was taken hostage by a religious spirit. It came right out of my fine upstanding "holified" Christian heritage. No way around it, I was disgustedly (yet happily) looking down on those less mature people who felt a need to do these light-hearted, two-inch-deep lyrics put to an obnoxious drumbeat and creative-less melody. More than that, I was looking down on any style and content of music that was not enjoyed by ME. Oh, the narcissistic pain of this humanity. Fortunately, this is not the end of the story. If it was, I no doubt would have become some small piano player working in some small church in some small town with an even smaller vision for the Kingdom. Nothing wrong with any of that if it's what God made you for. That was not the Father's plan for me. I just couldn't see it for all the religious baggage clouding my soul.

Jesus, help us.

And now, the rest of the story. I went home from the service and something was different, unsettled if you will, a feeling of "troubled" waters (in a good way), perhaps, in my spirit. I couldn't for the life of me remember how that opening song went, but I could not get it out of my head. I just had to find it somewhere and hear it again. Thankfully, I learned later that the service that night had been recorded and a cassette tape would be available soon after the conference had ended. If you're a young reader, ask your parents what cassettes tapes were. (Sheesh...feeling old about now.) I tell you the truth—I could not rest until I had that tape in my hand. What in the world was going on here!?! I will tell you the answer to that. God was doing a sovereign work in the heart of the religious boy from Kentucky. I have no other explanation. He was SETTING ME FREE from a religious spirit that had held me bound for all of my thirty years. And He was doing it in short order. I mean, like right now!

I took my newly acquired tape and my handy dandy portable cassette player and, feeling like I was not sure where my emotions were going, went up to the balcony of the church and proceeded to find a small room way back in the corner of the large building, sort of an attic behind the sanctuary, where man would seldom trod. I don't think there was even a light in the room. It was used to store some old Christmas decorations or other odds and ends that were no longer needed. I was almost fidgety as I popped the tape into the player and pushed the Play button. And then it happened. That's right—another Whoosh! moment, right there in the dark. I began to sing, and then I began to dance. You do realize I had never danced. We good Christian families would rather die than dance. "What if Jesus came back while you were dancing" was the age-old question. Not sure I ever really knew the answer to that one, but it was a good religious question nonetheless! Anyway, even though this was a spiritual dance, I'm trying to say that there was never any rug-cutting experience in these shoes, so calling it a dance was a stretch. But my feet could remain silent no longer. I was twirling, leaping, doing the Charismatic 2-step and just having a Holy Ghost time in the attic! At the end of the song…I let out a HUGE shout. Now, if you are not aware, God hath graced me with a very strong personal P.A. system, so when TMac shouts, the decibels are way up there. I let it rip. H A L L E L U J A H !!!!!!!

Saints, I wish I could communicate to you how the spirit of heaviness (which I KNOW was a religious spirit) totally leaped out of my being and flew away. It was AWESOME!!! I put everything within me into this shout and Whoosh!, the Spirit was all over me. I was forever a changed man. The Law of the Spirit of Life in Christ Jesus INSTANTLY set me free from the law of sin and death. How about that! What I did not know at the time was that God was about to open a door to work in a large charismatic church that would forever change my ministry. He had to prepare me for the next level…hence the introduction of victorious praise into my life. He does all things well and in perfect timing, does He not?

Wonderful people of the Kingdom, every day the enemy seeks

to kill, steal, or destroy your soul. It's a never-ending vicious cycle that he has commissioned his fallen angels to carry out. If he can instill a religious spirit in you, he may well have done, one, two, or all three of those things without you even knowing it. Religion is many times well-disguised, but its end is a big lie and looks nothing like relationship. Relationship is never disguisable, for those in true relationship can't hide their passionate love for Him and have nothing to hide anyway. Let others think what they may—it's just you and Jesus. You may have a long way to go in this, but I hope you are on your way to freedom, even if that starts with the reading of this book or listening to anointed music. However you get there, just get there. You'll be so glad you did!

Creation joins the heavens

to declare Your worth

I'll sing to You, give You my highest praise

And I'll proclaim,

how very, very great You are

He floods our soul with praise

The ancient of all days exalted King

His power fills our song

Brings forth the anthem strong

His greatness sing

CHAPTER SEVEN

Lu's Last Lullaby

> Stay alert! Watch out for your great enemy, the devil. He prowls around like a roaring lion, looking for someone to devour. (1 Peter 5:8, NLT)

I almost omitted this chapter from the book. I hate to even talk about our adversary and certainly do not wish to draw any attention to him whatsoever. Paul wrote much about the Christian walk, but very little was said about the creature who Paul said "masquerades as an angel of light." But if I do stick my head in spiritual sand, it won't change the fact that Satan, or Lucifer as he was formerly named, is a present enemy who, as warned by the scripture mentioned above, is on the prowl and not giving up.

I am a firm believer that if we do not know or understand our enemy, we will never defeat him in battle. The winners of wars throughout the ages have had cunning strategies to outsmart their opponents. They have studied them in detail in preparation for the conflict. The same must hold true for us as Christians. The work of Jesus at the cross has made it possible for constant victory over the one who will soon be crushed under our feet and has already been defeated, whether we see it in this present day or not.

Think about that last sentence: Satan has been beaten, yet we often live as though he is still in power over an area of our lives. Why? Because he is the great deceiver. He is the father of lies. Sadly, he has mastered this craft to perfection. But knowing this important fact should make us constantly on the alert and always seeking the truth, which is Jesus. So, I hope this chapter brings a clearer understanding of who this loser named Lucifer really is and puts him where he belongs...under our authority. Even as I type this, I can see him upset that I am truly including further information of his demise in this book. Feels pretty good just thinking about it! As has been my modus operandi throughout the book, let me share a couple of stories, okay maybe three...well, no more than four, that will hopefully drive my point home.

Faithful, He is faithful

There's no other that I can turn to

Faithful, He's been faithful

and He'll always be

He has crowned me with lovingkindness

And His mercies for me

are new each day

STORY #1. My friend Ken Groen, whom I have talked about numerous times in this book, has been a lifelong friend well beyond the time I worked for him as a young man. He, along with another friend and fellow worship leader, Paul Strang, and I have been a golfing trio that have rendezvoused from different regions of the country several times through the years for a golf and fellowship getaway that has provided many great memories and lots of laughter. Happily, aside from the very first of these outings in 1991, I have been the fortunate winner of the custom-made trophy each time we have played our hard-fought three-day tournament. That award is not as cherished as the 3 ½-inch trophy I won for a miniature golf tournament in my little town at the age of twelve, but it is indeed a fun thing to occasionally look at and reminisce with fondness. Ken has always been a good sport in losing, which makes the rest of this story so ironic.

He and I were on vacation with our wives in Hawaii several years ago. We carved out a day to play golf on one of the beautiful ocean-lined courses in Maui. The competition is friendly, but always present, even through a plethora of subjects while riding in the golf cart together throughout the four-hour activity. This game went about like all the other games of the past many years we have been playing, meaning, I was winning. The eighteenth and final hole arrived, and victory was sure, as I had a seven stroke lead. I think Ken had peacefully resigned to losing again. Suddenly, as if I was acting out a scene from an unlikely sports comeback movie, the wheels came off. I couldn't hit the ocean from the beach! My drive went far to the right; my second, third, and fourth shots were pathetic duffs. Meanwhile Ken stayed in the fairway and watched my shenanigans continue as he easily made his way to the green and waited. By the sixth attempt at advancing my ball with any coordination at all, laughter had now crept into my soul. A few more errant swings and I finally made it to the green, only to three-putt to finish the game one stroke behind Ken. He was ecstatic. Normally I am one of the most competitive people you will ever meet in your lifetime, but that day I couldn't help but rejoice with my friend over his most surprising victory. I suppose had it been the regular threesome tournament we were accustomed to playing, there would have been only frustration and humiliation, but not today. As much as I hate to lose, I felt happiness for my buddy.

Now, fast-forwarding to a time probably a year or more later, I was lying awake in my bed very early one morning. As was the norm, when I wake up my brain goes immediately into action. For some reason on this morning my mind went back to the Maui golf game. I began reliving the eighteenth hole debacle and had to keep myself from chuckling out loud so as not to awaken my wife. I spent several moments in thought of how I had surrendered a seemingly sure victory. Then, out of nowhere, as I turned over from my left side to my right, a nearly audible and dreadful voice spoke to me, saying, "You will never finish this race." My merriment of the moment turned to an instant gasp and I quickly broke out in cold sweat! Fear gripped my heart like never before. I am convinced that Satan himself made a visit to my bedroom that day. It rocked me…and rocked me hard. We will revisit this later.

> *Morning dew, gentle breeze*
> *As I walk down the lane with Him*
> *And He softly whispers "Son I love you"*
> *And my heart becomes brand new again,*
> *my God, my friend*

STORY #2. On my most recent album, as I was putting together a song list for what would be included, I was drawn to a tune—one I did not write—called "No Longer Slaves." You may have well heard this song, as a couple of years ago it was voted the contemporary Christian song of the year. The two-line repeated chorus goes like this: "I'm no longer a slave to fear; I am a child of God." Most of the music on my albums is not contemporary, and is not old school, it's just…me. Not sure how else to explain it. So, this was a bit of a stretch, but I liked the Spirit's touch on it and felt like it would make an important statement on this album, as I sought the Lord for direction. Probably less than two weeks later, I was awakened out of a deep sleep, again in the early morning hours shortly after daybreak. This time as I opened my eyes there was a presence, a dark ominous skeleton-like presence hovering just up and to the right of me. I sort of fiercely waved my hand in its direction while shouting "Go!" That ugly and hateful thing left as quickly as it came. I lay in bed, heart pounding for several minutes. Later that day I was recounting the moment when the Holy Spirit whispered, "It's because of the song." I instantly knew He meant "No Longer Slaves." I had hit a nerve in the enemy's camp by deciding to record that song in our live Trinidad concert. If you've heard the recording, you know the power and deliverance from fear that has accompanied the singing and my exhortation after the song's end. It was a special moment—one of several on the CD. We will also revisit this in a few minutes.

STORY #3. My youngest son Drew received a bicycle for Christmas when he was twelve. It was a beauty; shiny blue and silver, twenty-one speeds, dual brakes, the works! Drew was pumped. He had been riding a bike for several years already, so looking at the directions seemed pointless. Later that day he went riding with a buddy of his as we were preparing to have dinner with friends at our house. Then the phone rang. Long story short, Drew had applied the front and rear brakes at the same time—something that should never be done on this type of a bicycle, and locked the wheels, throwing him over the top of the bike and hurling him several feet in the air, finally landing on the pavement. He came down on his skinny little left arm, causing a compound fracture. Oh friends, what a mess that arm was. I could literally see bone sticking out at two different points.

To this day it was probably my worst memory of fatherhood. How I ached for my son. The next afternoon after Drew's complex surgery, he was home lying on the living room couch. As I walked by him, I heard a voice. Thankfully this time it was God's. He simply said this to me, "Satan sought your son's life yesterday." The reality of the accident hit me all over again. God showed me how angel intervention had brought Drew's body down just a short distance from a major thoroughfare. Losing a son like this would have been a pain greater than I think I could have withstood; it surely would have drastically affected my life and ministry forever.

So, there you have three stories involving the enemy of our soul. There are lessons to be learned from all three. The first part of John 10:10 provides us with perhaps the greatest insight of knowledge regarding Satan's sole purpose: "The thief comes only to steal, kill, and destroy…" Key operative word here is "only." This is the way Lucifer works; he will try to steal from you; if he can't do that he will try to kill you; if he can't do that he will try to destroy you. If that doesn't work he will try to steal from you again, and on and on the vicious wheel turns. His plan is simple and lifelong—to do ONLY those three things. He is relentless, and we need to be the same in our defense against his onslaught.

Turn my eyes to You O Lord

Help my heart to trust You more

Rain Your healing love upon my soul

Turn my eyes to You alone

Looking at Story #1, I interpreted his attack that said I would never finish this race as meaning I wouldn't continue to serve God all the days of my life. That's how it felt. Of course, he knows that I have been a devout follower of Christ since I was a child, and so that's where he attacked. I've had ups and downs in life—some of the downs have been really bad; but I have never considered turning away from my relationship with God. Ole slew foot picked the wrong part of my walk to attack. He overplayed his hand again. He usually does. I have settled in my heart that the Word of God is true and I am His child forever. Period. End of debate. I already shared in chapter 3 about the suicide spirit I had to battle one night during a difficult season. That night was the carefully crafted culmination of the threat he sent my way two years previous while I lay in bed back on that memorable morning I told you about. But he failed, didn't he? This you can count on. Lu is a liar, plain and simple. He is the father of lies. When he prophesied my doom to me that morning, he was lying. It's up to us to recognize and cast out the imagination that will want to give life to the lie. The truth sets us free. Renew your mind daily and know that you know who you are in Christ. Expose the lie and throw it back on him. What a creep!

Looking at Story #2, somehow the enemy must have known how powerful that song "No Longer Slaves" was going to be on the new CD. He surely did not want me messing with the spirit of fear. Incidentally, I personally believe that fear is the greatest antichrist spirit on the earth today. It will make you do what you don't want to do and keep you from doing exactly what you want to do, and more importantly, what God wants you to do. When

I reentered ministry eight years ago, right before I walked on to the platform, a spirit of fear suddenly gripped my heart. That has never happened to me in my life. It was again totally sent from the pits of Hell. It couldn't have come from anywhere else. So, when I selected this song to bring freedom to God's kids from that crippling spirit, Satan decided to spring it on me as I shared above. How ironic that as soon as I said GO!, the evil presence immediately disappeared. Does that tell you anything? The power of life and death is in the tongue, saints. The authority of the believer is in the tongue. Revelation 12:11 promises that victory over Satan comes through the blood of the Lamb and the words of our mouth. Declare your authority over him who is under our feet. Keep him right there, every day. It's where he belongs.

Story #3 reveals just how devious and wretchedly awful our enemy is. He will steal the most precious thing from you if you allow him to take residence in your heart or home. My children are the three greatest inheritances God has given me over the past thirty-seven years. They mean the world to me. I'm so proud of each one of them, simply because they are my sons, and they love and faithfully serve the same God that I do. Those two things are at the apex of life for me. So, if our adversary can't get to us at a particular time, he will try to steal that which is precious to our hearts. He is pure trash...even smellier than trash. We need to learn to hate him more every day. Ask God to give you power to hate Lu. He deserves every hatred. Thankfully, in this case, I have no doubt that angels were in attendance around Drew's bike and preserved his life. Oh, how we need that divine help from on high. What a gift His angels are to His children.

Friends, we must be wise as serpents and gentle as doves in this day and age. This is the last hurrah for the prince of the power of the air. This is his final lullaby. He's going to try to sing you to sleep in his deception. The Word says he disguises himself as an angel of light. I concur. He's doing that very thing in churches across our land. He's going to pull out every trick in the book to try to bring many more lost souls and even some found ones into eternity with him if he can. Sometimes when you think you've won, he comes back around again.

Permit me to share just one more brief story. It happened in Kalispell, Montana, several years ago. I was asked to lead worship for the dedication and groundbreaking for a new prayer center there. It was a fantastic vision, and as the leader of that vision spoke at the Saturday afternoon dedication service, there was an unusual intensity of the Holy Spirit that began to slowly rise, almost methodically throughout the service. I was to lead worship after the message on that day. By the time it was my turn, there was a heaviness (the good kind) sitting on that place. I got up and began to sing "Oh the Glory of Your Presence," a song that many have heard on our "Sound of Heaven" CD. The problem was, the glory was so overwhelming that I sang the first phrase and then broke down for a moment, having to regather myself while skipping the second phrase. I got my composure back to sing the third phrase, and then He hit me again and I couldn't sing the next line. By the end of the song, I was on the carpet, face down, lost in weeping as the Spirit just flooded that place with Himself. Others were in the same mode. It was one of the holiest moments in recent memory of my life. That signified to me that God was all over this vision, and great things were about to take place in the unlikely town of Kalispell.

I wish that was the end or maybe the beginning of the story. It is not. For reasons unknown to me, there is no prayer center today. The first hole has not been dug. I can only conclude that the enemy has thrown a wrench into things and shut everything down. Perhaps it will be resurrected under different leadership at a different time. I pray so. But Lu has done a number on somebody. Upon checking the progress of this story, I found out today that there are a number of prayer groups now meeting in homes. I rejoice in that, but I can't help wondering if this was the original plan of God because of what so many experienced that day, including me. I highly doubt it.

This type of story can be repeated in cities around the world. Great vision starts—the enemy comes in like a flood, and then the vision dies. How many times have you heard that? My guess is many. We're having to operate for a little longer on his turf. He knows his time is short. Let us be a wise people. Too much gullibility exists in the body of Christ. Way too much. That's why charlatans have a field day with so many in the church. Stupid sheep do whatever the slickest shepherd tells them. It breaks my heart. We should all make the reading of Proverbs a daily, weekly, and monthly habit. You can't get too much of God's wisdom! Let us be sharp in our discernment in these end-times. Try the spirits and see if they are of God. Renew your minds...daily. Victory is ahead. Let's march on together. It says in 2 Timothy 1:7: "For the Spirit God gave us does not make us timid, but gives us power, love and self-discipline." AMEN!

CHAPTER EIGHT

A Deposit That Remains

For all creation, gazing eagerly as if with outstretched neck, is waiting and longing to see the manifestation of the sons of God. (Romans 8:19, Weymouth New Testament)

As you may have noticed in the opening pages, this book is dedicated to my oldest brother, Edward. This chapter will be the same…dedicated to him. Ed and I became close to each other, really for the first time, ten years ago when I went through an aforementioned dark and very difficult season of life. He remained consistent in loving me when I was struggling to be lovable to anyone. He did not judge…what a concept. Friends, let me say if there is an ounce of judgment in your heart toward others, please stop. Two reasons: first, Jesus said, "Don't judge, or you're asking for it"; second, you simply are not the one wearing the judge's robe. Why did Jesus tell us not to judge? Because we are clueless to another man's walk. This includes family, friends, sports heroes, political figures, ministerial superstars, and the like. Just stop. You will lead a more peaceful life and be a far more pleasurable creation to God when you do.

So, Ed was there for me. God probably knew I would need a big brother when life changed as drastically as it did. There were a few others to whom I had no connection that reached out to me, but that was not going to be a path I could afford to take at the time. I needed affirming love from people who had a vested interest in me or at least a relationship with me. Ed was that. We've been close since that time, and for the past several years we had been weekly texting or Skyping pals until just this past May of 2018—when from a very bad heart with complications from diabetes, he breathed his last breath in St. Louis and his next breath in Glory. I miss him every day, and have wanted to type a "hey, how's your week going?" to him a hundred times already. I'm sure his family feels the same. His wife, Teresa, lost her love and her best friend in a single moment. His three daughters lost their hero. Life is hard...yet God remains good all the time despite the hard times we have to face in life.

Ed's life and walk were quiet in nature. He was never flashy, couldn't care less about style or affluence, and lived what he believed. He is included as the lead story in this chapter for one reason...throughout his life he made spiritual deposits that remained, and he was a pretty darn good example to his little brother. Funny how life is; much of what I learned about these deposits was only discovered after he died and the news of his passing went out through the world of email, Facebook, and the like. A day or two later I read comments from former students of his when he was a philosophy professor at Evangel College (now Evangel University). Apparently, his class was one that everybody wanted to be in. He had developed a reputation in his short time there for teaching his classes how to critically think about the Word of God. I have a friend who pastors a large church in Dayton, Ohio. He was one of Ed's students. He would testify today how what Ed taught him has helped him in studying the Word forty years later. Our own father attended my brother's class one day while visiting the school campus. Ed found him at the water fountain after the conclusion of the class, in tears, obviously moved by the depth of Ed's teaching. "I never knew this," Dad lamented. "I've served God my whole life and never heard anything like this." It was Spirit-infused teaching. How do I know this? Because the Spirit brings LIFE!

If you haven't caught that underlying theme of this book yet, catch it now. This earth belongs to God and the fullness thereof. When we connect to the Holy Spirit, we instantly align ourselves with the purpose and fullness of God in His creation. It's a slam dunk! Ed was giving his students life as they were learning more about God. You hear about it from various campuses—some Christian and some secular. One professor will have a waiting list for his classes. He's got something they thirst for. This reminds me of the last scene in "Mr. Holland's Opus," when everyone the band director touched over thirty years of teaching showed up to honor him at his retirement. I have watched that scene at least a dozen times and still cry every time. It just hits me where I live.

A fulfilled life includes impacting other lives. The man who spoke at my brother's funeral is Timothy Best, a Major in the Salvation Army. Ed spent thirteen years as a staff member of that organization. Tim began his remarks by saying something to the nature of, "People know me as a Major with The Salvation Army. That sounds nice, but what I really am is a former alcoholic and cocaine addict from the streets of Detroit that Dr. Ed counseled to physical and spiritual health." Friends, that's a deposit that remained. That's a Mr. Holland moment. Ed went on to train Tim and many others like him so that they could in turn help many more. Great legacy. I'm proud of my big brother.

Hearing and following the Spirit's voice is key in making lasting deposits in people's lives. If our ear is tuned to His voice, He will whisper something at the right time for the right situation. An illustration of this goes as follows: a pastor of a tiny church in rural Scotland one morning felt directed by the Holy Spirit to walk several miles into town, but he didn't know why. The round trip would take him a good part of the day, yet he felt strongly that he needed to be obedient to the voice that was so familiar. So off he went. When he finally reached the outskirts of town, he came upon a stretch of sidewalk in front of a section of row houses, as they are called in Europe. Those are small homes attached by a common wall, sort of what we might call townhomes here, but there are many stacked one after the other in a row. Got it? Anyway, as he approached the entrance to the town, praying in the Spirit, he felt led to stop and sing. "Amazing Grace" was what came to him, so he sang...all four verses. He felt a bit strange doing it, but this entire trip seemed a bit odd, so why not just go with the flow, he thought. After he completed the song, the burden lifted. He turned around and went home. Different kind of day, but an obedient one. Many years later the pastor heard of a well-known evangelist who was coming to his area to hold a large crusade. The humble Scottish preacher had always wanted to hear this man in person, so he gathered the family, found some transportation, and made his way to the auditorium where the meeting was to be held. Getting there rather late they had to sit in the balcony. No worries, at least they had made it. Finally, after the music portion of the meeting was finished, the evangelist was introduced. He thanked those in charge for sponsoring the special meeting and then went on to tell the overflow crowd how this town meant so much to him personally, for it was there in an upstairs open-windowed room that he lay dying in bed without knowing God. One day someone began to sing "Amazing Grace, how sweet the sound, that saved a wretch like me." He went on to say that God touched his body, raised him up, and he surrendered his heart to Jesus that day. (I'm crying again, and I've told this story a thousand times!) People of God, THIS IS LIFE! One man can touch one man who can touch an entire nation. The little Scottish nobody preacher made a deposit that remained! And he made a deposit so strongly connected with the presence of God that it raised up a dying man and convicted his heart to salvation. That's Power. That's obedience. That's Jesus.

There are two types of people in the world—givers and takers. Shortly after you read that last sentence you knew which one of those you are, if you are honest with yourself. When I had a large staff working for me in Colorado several years ago, I would periodically ask them, "Are you giving more than you're receiving? If you are, then you're more blessed." I ask you, the reader, the same question. And if you're more of a taker than a giver, then I encourage you to do an about-face. My greatest joy is found in giving, no matter what it is I'm giving. Don't get me wrong, it's expensive. Whether it's money, friendship, love, or time, it's expensive. But all of God's ways are pricey. Those are the best kind because they bring the best rewards. I love to give. It's my best love language.

Making a deposit that remains has become the theme of my

pre-service prayer each time I minister nowadays. I have no desire to do just another concert. I must find Him somewhere in that service and impart Him to the people. I always wait for what I hope will be the felt transfer of the anointing from the platform to the pew. If it doesn't happen, it doesn't happen. Much of that is out of my hands anyway, but I want to keep my heart pure and open to His leading so that what happens in that service remains in the hearts of the people long after Liz and I have departed. It should be what ministry is all about anyway. So many make it about themselves instead of Him or His people. Often well disguised, there are wolves in sheep's clothing all around us. I was so repulsed by one "up and coming" evangelist a few years ago, I grabbed Liz and we left only a few minutes into his manipulative message. That did not set well with leadership, who had brought me in for the worship portion of the conference, but I could not allow our spirits to be a part of the shenanigans done in the name of Christ. It sickens me.

The body of Christ is such a gullible people. Make no mistake about it. I pray my own motives are always singular—to bring the presence of Jesus to every person I minister to. That's what I know the CDs have done, and I pray they are still continuing to do around the world. To have this motive, there's always a high price to pay. No one really understands the agonizing that goes into my recording projects or the way I am forced to guard my heart as I travel around the world. I say no to an awful lot of invitations. Much discernment is needed. When I'm making CDs, I've always compared it to having a baby (like I would know what THAT feels like) because the process is usually about nine months long, and there's much morning sickness, labor pains galore, and finally delivery. If I was only representing myself and wanted to make some good music, that would be one thing. But because I represent the Chief Musician and carry a precious anointing that I have seen change people's lives for so long now, the responsibility is great, and the Lord requires much out of this clay vessel. Every time I complete a new CD (there are something like eighteen of them out there now) I wonder if it will be my last. I just feel so spent. That's probably how I should feel. But I always know the stamp of the Holy Spirit comes down, as if to say, "It's done, it's mine and the enemy can never steal it." I love that thought. Then at the right time God puts a new burden in my heart for a new avenue of worship. It does take time, though. Tough to get pregnant right after having a baby anyway, right, ladies?

Looking at the Biblical characters, they were all about making deposits that remained. Oh, they may not have started out that way; in fact, many of them surely were not of that desire at all. Jonah comes to mind right off the top of my head. He wanted nothing to do with God's call. And then there's Moses, who thought of several excuses of why he couldn't do the will of God. Of course, Paul was an enemy of the cross in his early days, so his efforts were anti-everything that's good. James and John were more concerned with position than servanthood. But when all of these collective hearts experienced the touch of God and realized the high calling of God, then making deposits that remained was all they cared about from then on in their lives. When you have a "meeting" with the living God, your heart will never be the same. This brings me to the night that a deposit was made from heaven into my soul that remains to this day. It was a night to remember.

I was just out of high school, attending a summer youth camp with my church. At the end of the service we were instructed to pair off in twos and go seek the Lord for a season. Leon Hunt was my prayer buddy, and we went to kneel together at a picnic table out on the grounds of the camp. After we had been praying for a short time, I started to feel something I had never felt before. Mind you, I had felt His presence many times before, as I have already described. But tonight was different...almost scary, in a good way. As we waited on the Lord, He began to...umm...sort of sit on me with His presence. Have you heard the phrase "the weight of His glory"? Well, this was certainly that. His glory, His manifest presence, was so heavy upon me I could not physically lift my head. It was as if a cloud type of thing was forcing it to stay bowed down practically to the ground. This went on for over an hour! I told Leon to go get the pastor. He did so, and when Ken came and stood over me, he helped interpret what God was doing with me that night. "Terry, I think the Lord is setting you apart for ministry. He's putting His hand on you," Ken said. I knew that had to be it as soon as he said it. I've never before or after felt an intensity of that level, and I've had some doozy visitations in my life. That night He gave me a vision of leading thousands of people with their hands raised in worship to the Lord. That vision was a bit odd, since I was nothing but an organist in a small church. But God.

That scene would be realized some twenty-eight years later when I stood before a crowd of 18,000 people as a guest minister at Benny Hinn's crusade in Shreveport, Louisiana. At one point during my fifty-minute worship time that was supposed to only last twenty minutes, God told me to open my eyes. It happened to be during a time when the song of the Lord had broken out among the people. I opened my eyes and saw exactly what my vision had been twenty-eight years before. Wow. The throng of people were LOST in the glory of God. You had to be there to know what I mean. It was off the charts. Benny later told me his crusades have never gone to that level in the Spirit realm. So, all of that and everything that has happened since in my ministry has been a result of a very important deposit of the glory of God, deep into my spirit way back at a picnic table in 1973. That deposit remains today. I'm lost without it...without Him. Yes, meeting with God changes everything. That's what spending time in His presence is all about. I am so grateful for every one of those connections throughout my life, and I hope there are dozens more before my life is done. Every time we get close to Him, we get filled with Him so that we can make a deposit from Him that remains in someone else's life. My son is a staff pastor at a large church in Ft. Collins, Colorado. Occasionally he is asked to preach the weekend message. We usually chat about his topic, and before the conversation has ended I always ask him, "What is the ONE THING you are going to say that will stay with the people for the rest of their lives?" It's something I wish all preachers would consider. I say this because I can recall very little of the thousands of sermons I've heard over the course of my life. When we are in His presence, He will reveal to us that one thing that will remain. That's really all that matters. Live to give and give your best.

Two days ago, I spoke on this very subject at a local church here in the DFW area. I challenged people to make a difference, to make a deposit in their neighborhood, their market place, their schools, etc. Today one of Liz's and my good friends, Amber, who was in that service, did just that. Long story short, she was conducting a business transaction with an unsaved man who was burdened about his mom, who had been diagnosed with cancer. Amber decided to make a deposit, so she stepped out in faith with this total stranger and prayed that the doctor's report would change. She told the man she was going to believe God's report for his mother. Later today the man sent her a text saying, "You must really know how to pray. New X-rays were taken this afternoon—there's NO CANCER!"

Amber made a deposit. More than that, she was a channel for God's power. Now THAT'S some deposit to make. Perhaps the Kingdom will gain several souls from this unmistakable visit of God's power to the human body. This is what it's all about. You can do it too. Listen for the whisper of the Holy Spirit, then take a step of faith. Whatever He says to you, do it. You might be surprised at the results!

I love Your presence Lord

Your beauty I adore

Your glory You outpour

I love Your presence Lord

CHAPTER NINE

Can You Hear the Sound of Heaven?

Then I heard something like the voice of a great multitude and like the sound of many waters and like the sound of mighty peals of thunder, saying, "Hallelujah! For the Lord our God, the Almighty, reigns. (Revelation 19:6, NASB)

Heaven—the ultimate worship arena; the goal and final destination for every true believer and follower of Christ. The place where there is no sorrow, no failure, no jealousy, no competition, and a ton of other "nos." But more importantly, a place where we will finally see our Savior face to face. When you hear about people seeing Jesus in bodily form on the earth, be very skeptical. They have not. They may have seen an angel, but they did not see Jesus. He is IN heaven at the Father's right hand, and He will STAY in heaven until the Father gives Him the OK to return for His bride. Whether that happens pre-, mid-, or post-tribulation is a discussion that seems to take place in each generation since He ascended over 2000 years ago. But rest assured—you won't see Him until you see Him on that very important day. If that statement offends the Crazomatics, then forgive me. Just the facts here.

The title of this chapter, as many of the readers of this book know well already, is the first line of perhaps the second most sung song of my own compositions around the world... "Holy Are You Lord." One of my earlier songs, "I Sing Praises," would have to be the most popular of the tunes God has given me over the years, as it is now sung in just about every language and people known to man. That's another story for another day, but suffice to say the Chief Musician has done more with that little chorus than I ever thought possible. However, this chapter is about the former song mentioned, as it has probably brought a "Presence" experience to more people on the earth than all my other songs put together since I penned it in 1999. It's a "Heavensong"; I don't know how else to describe it. If I ever write a second book, it will probably be a compilation of the stories behind the songs. I will save further description of this for that publication if, and when, it happens. For now, I want to focus on the sound of heaven.

Many years ago I had a colleague, David Morris, who became a good friend. David was a worship leader at the church I attended in Colorado Springs, and we spent many hours over many lunches together during that season of life. Sadly, David lost a battle with cancer and graduated far too early to his eternal reward; well, early as far as friends and family were concerned. I would suspect David was happy to receive his crown and begin his trouble-free life with Jesus...and I KNOW he would not exchange it for anything on this piece of clay now that he's won his race and made it home. So, several months after David's passing, I had a dream one night. That's normally no big deal to me because I must dream more than anybody in the history of the world—or so it seems. But this dream was different, a real keeper that is still clear to me today. David was sent back to earth to do something that was left unfinished when he first departed. I have no idea what it was, but I remember his appearance very well in the dream. He wore a medium blue blazer, and had a flawless olive-skinned face, which featured the most peaceful and perfect look in his eyes I had ever seen. In my dream it appeared David did not have much time to talk with me. He walked by me and acknowledged me with a "Hey, Ter, how's it going?" I was so happy to see him again I exuberantly shouted his name, as anyone can imagine they would. I realized he was in a hurry, so as he walked on by I said to him, "Hey, man, what's it like?" Of course, you know what I was talking about and so did David. He instantly replied, "Perfected praise... perfected praise, Ter...it's really cool." (I can SO hear him say that even as I type this.) And with that he was gone. End of dream.

I remember how several months after that I was sharing this dream while teaching at a worship seminar, when all of a sudden the worship scene of heaven hit me like a ton of bricks. Another Whoosh! moment was upon me. I wept at the revelation of how perfect the praise was coming from the throne. I had totally lost control of myself while trying to teach. I can't say that has ever happened before or since that day. It was a wild moment in the Spirit. Somehow, God chose that particular time to reveal just what heaven's worship scene is like. I never saw it when the dream happened. He had to revisit me with the whole idea a second time. Think about it. Perfect praise coming from perfect vessels in a perfect setting to exalt a perfect Lord. It's the perfect vessels part that really hit me that day. What a sound we will make when every encumbrance has fallen off our glorified beings. What a sound when our voices are joined with a vocal quality unlike we have ever heard on the earth. What a sound when we worship with the saints from all the ages. That is going to be something.

On three occasions in the past I have been a guest minister at the Brooklyn Tabernacle. This is a special place that God has set apart as a gift to all who enter there. The church is a very old and beautiful converted theatre where Broadway-type plays used to happen. Along with the 4,000-seat sanctuary, there are six floors in the building where the administrative offices are located. Pastor Jim Cymbala's office is up on the top floor. On that Sunday evening when I was to minister, he and I were talking, and then he said, "Come on, the service has started." We made our way down the elevator to the main floor. As we were walking toward the double-door entrance to the sanctuary, I could already hear the 200-voice choir and the full house of worshipers singing, "Victory is mine, victory is mine, victory today is mine…" It's a song that really rocks, and believe me, this place was rockin'! I remember wishing Pastor Jim would walk faster because I couldn't wait to get into that atmosphere. Such life, such electricity, such heaven!

That scene is a snapshot of what it must be like to enter the worship arena of heaven. Can you imagine a full orchestra of perfectly tuned instruments with every player being fully anointed of the Holy Spirit, oil dripping off the violin bows, trumpets playing in perfect harmony covering octaves above and below what we have heard down here; sounds that cut through the atmosphere with the power of God. WOW! Think of the angelic choir, thousands and thousands and ten thousand times ten thousand. By the way, if we are to literally interpret that verse in Revelation, that total would be over 100 million voices. WOW AGAIN!!! And ohhh, does heaven rock! Not a quiet place at all—sorry for you whispering worshipers. It's like the sound of MANY RUSHING WATERS AND PEELS OF THUNDER. Crash! Boom! Crash some more! It's one LOUD place, saints. You're gonna love it—even if you currently like it quiet in church!

I have no idea how many times I have sung "Holy Are You Lord" over the past twenty years in my concerts, but it must be over a thousand by now, since it seems to be a song that many are waiting for each time I minister. Often when I'm singing I see my grandfather, who was himself a Pentecostal pioneer in New York state a hundred years ago, standing next to my dad, who also loved to worship, as they lift their voices together in praise to their King. In the past couple of months, I have seen my brother joining them around the throne. Sometimes I still get choked up at the very thought of this and cannot wait to be a part of that scene, perhaps very soon if the present world conditions are any indicator. I often talk about that first worship service in heaven and how it will take our celestial breath away as we join the song for the first time.

So, as this and the following closing chapter of this book are crafted to be more of "How to" than testimonial in nature, let me ask you this very simple yet pointed question...can you hear the sound of heaven? I mean, can YOU hear the sound of heaven? When you listen to anointed music, does something happen inside your spirit that instantly connects your spirit with His, or is it just a pleasant experience that fills your day? Some of you know my assistant, Pat Penn, who has served our ministry for several years.

I remember Pat saying how for the longest time she listened to the music without ever truly hearing or feeling the worship. Then one day it hit her in a very direct way, and she's been a different worshiper since that time. That's what I'm talking about. I have had dozens of people tell me the very same thing.

That's where God desires every one of us to live...connected to His Spirit. I have led countless hundreds of thousands in worship over the years. Some of them are instantly in His presence in my services, some of them come along at a slower pace to finally find God in the music, and some never come close to getting there. Of course, as a servant of the Most High, I want for every person who has taken the time to come out to a concert to receive the reward of His presence, whether for thirty seconds or thirty minutes. I wish I had a magic button to push to help you get there. Unfortunately, I'm just the piano player. On that note, years ago God made it clear..."You just take care of Terry worshiping, and I will take care of my people." Yes sir, instructions received and understood. Roger Wilco!

The Secret Place of His Spirit

Sometimes with all the distractions of life we forget that we are spirit beings. As the adage goes, I AM a spirit; I HAVE a soul; and I LIVE in a body. That's a good thing to remind ourselves during the ups and downs of life. When our time here is over, two of those three attributes will no longer come into play. However, the spirit shall remain.

Bodies will eventually be new, and souls will be restored to perfection, but we must give proper attention to this thing that is our spirit. That's where God dwells. Our soul (mind, will, and emotions) cannot relate to our spirit. In fact, Scripture tells us they are big-time enemies. I have certainly seen that throughout my own journey. I'm sure you have too. When we give in to our flesh and do only what our soul dictates, we as believers are not fulfilling the higher calling of God, and truth be told, we're not finding true fulfillment at all. We cannot...we were made to be bondservants with Jesus after we received Him as Savior. The selfish soul wants what it wants, and wants it now. The yielded spirit waits for God and is content when He comes and completes the good work He has begun. It's an entirely different thought process, and every time I choose that process I am a happier and much more peaceful man. It's a daily challenge and sometimes a daily struggle. The Christian life...not for sissies!

Looking at how our heroes of the Bible lived, I think of John, the "I John" from Revelation. Most scholars think he was the same John as the Apostle in the book of John. That makes the most sense to me too. Of course, He wasn't commissioned to write the finale of the Bible. He just wrote what he saw, and God took care of the rest. Here is the key to John and the book of Revelation: chapter one, verse ten... "I was in the Spirit on the Lord's day." This, my fine feathered friends, was the ONLY prerequisite needed to receive and write twenty-two chapters of the last chunk of the best-selling book of all time, as vital two thousand years later as it was the day ol' Johnny grabbed his Montblanc pen and his Ritz Carlton notepad and began to jot down what he had seen as he lay comfortably on his penthouse lanai overlooking the ocean.

Yeah, right. Suffering in dismal conditions on the island of Patmos, think of the weight of those nine decisive words…"I was in the Spirit on the Lord's day." John, advanced in years, left all the pain and distractions behind on a Sunday morning as he pressed into the realm of the Spirit. Once he was there the download commenced, and this most intriguing book of the New Testament was born. I have often wondered how long John was "out" in the Spirit to have the detailed vision we have read. Could have been a few minutes, could have been a few days for all I know. But rest assured he was in the manifest presence of God when it all came down. He was hearing the sound for sure. He was even seeing things as they were to come.

You may have distractions hitting you from every direction. You may have physical pain in your body or spiritual pain in your heart. Lay it aside and press into Him, whatever that means to you. Psalm 91 tells us that he who dwells in the secret place shall abide under the shadow of God. What a great place to be. We need to go there far more often than we do. He's always waiting.

Have you ever had a vision? I know many people have had awesomely detailed visions. Without a doubt they were in the Spirit when it happened. I guess I have kind of, sort of, had a vision, as I shared what I saw the night God called me to ministry back in chapter 8 of this book. I'm hesitant to call it a full-blown vision because of how brief it was, along with no details to speak of, hence the "kind of, sort of" appraisal. It was nothing like many I have heard, but it was real as the Spirit brooded over me. According to Scripture, young men see visions and old men dream dreams. Although I remember some pointed spiritual dreams in my youth, I'm afraid I qualify more for that latter category these days. So, the Lord is welcome to dream a little dream with me!

It's strange though; there was a five-year period when I had many spiritual dreams. It's not a coincidence that I was working in a charismatic church at that time that talked about such things quite often. When one is exposed to more knowledge and discourse about something, it becomes more a part of the subconscious, and/or more a part of one's soul or spirit. On the practical side of thinking, it only makes sense that once it's in there, it has the opportunity to manifest itself in a dream or vision. I had some incredible spiritual dreams during that season of life. Prophetic victories and warnings were fairly common.

So much is available to any who walk in step and listen closely to His voice. My wife, Liz, often has dreams of her two children. Those dreams seem to ALWAYS coordinate with what's going on in their lives, even though she knows nothing of it at the time. Pretty amazing stuff. Whether you are a younger or older reader of this book, there's a good chance you can have a vision or dream about spiritual matters or something significant if you do this one important thing…ask God for it. Profound, isn't it? Ask the Father to use you in this way and watch Him grant the desires of your heart. Believe and you will receive. I think it really is that simple. You may find yourself in the worship arena of heaven as I did when I wrote "Holy Are You Lord." You may find yourself alone in the Holy of Holies with Jehovah. Wherever He takes you, I'm confident you will know Him a bit better when you return.

You and I need to hear the sound of heaven when we worship. That's why so many play my CDs over and over. There are moments when you can hear it...the sound, the unmistakable sound. Beyond that, you and I need to find ourselves "in the Spirit on the Lord's day." That means laying everything else down, including the sin that so easily besets us. God has no desire to speak to us when our hearts are divided and we're playing both sides of the fence in our lives, even if the other side is a very small part of us, which it usually is for the believer. He wants everything. He always has, and He always will. He told me long ago He will only share certain mysteries with me when I am in the holy place with Him. That is consistent with who He is and how He operates. Amazing God. With all the pressures of life seemingly begging for our attention and our strength, may His Holy Spirit help us to steal away with Him and lay it all down in worship. As I said before, He's always waiting. Let's go.

Lord You are holy, so very holy
All of creation will bow and worship
now our Father, Creator,
Master and Savior
Reign in majesty for all to see,
Lord You are holy, Lord You are holy
Worthy of glory and praise
all our days oh Lord.

CHAPTER TEN

Finally

I give thanks to you, O Lord my God, with my whole heart, and I will glorify your name forever. (Psalm 86:12, ESV)

I had originally chosen "Finally" as the chapter title, then I changed it to "All the Glory," endeavoring to once again highlight the special CD that I hope you have heard, and also to give God glory for this piece of work. Last week my wife said, "you should have called the book 'Finally,' since it's been so long in coming. That made me think twice about the change in direction for this chapter. Then a few days later I met with a pastor friend and told her I was writing a book. She instantly replied, "Finally!" That sort of sealed it. So, we have finally reached the final chapter of a book that is finally being written by this worship leader, who has some final thoughts for you to consider...finally.

Once again, I remind you that this entire deal is Yahweh's...not just the book—but all we know as life. The earth and everything in it—all exists for His glory. Every visitation of the His presence mentioned in these ten chapters is the result of His Spirit by His grace being poured out in unusual ways upon His people. Now to those of you who are reading this and have never had one of these "Whoosh" moments mentioned often during these pages, do not be dismayed. It shall yet come upon thee if you want Him in that dimension and seek Him with all your heart. And rest assured that although the Scripture admonishes us to "stir up the gifts," you cannot stir yourself up to one of these visitations. It definitely is a work of the Spirit in your heart that will bring it about. So, don't sweat it. Just earnestly ask Him for it, believe it will come to you, and wait for it to happen as you seek His face. You're obviously reading this book because you have interest in more of His Spirit invading your life. This is a good thing. Let's look at some critical points to help in our search for finding these special connections with the King of glory.

1. BE DOERS, NOT HEARERS ONLY. This was a big step I took when I came out of denominationalism in the mid-80s. The charismatic movement introduced me to actually believing and doing the Word of God. What a concept! One of those aspects was everyday prayer. Not the kneel down and give God fifteen minutes of attention, although there's nothing wrong with that. But, being more comfortable with instant prayer. I like what Paul says to us in 1 Thessalonians: 5:16-18: "Rejoice always, pray without ceasing, give thanks in all circumstances; for this is the will of God in Christ Jesus for you" (Berean Study Bible). I'm starting to just up and pray when someone tells me of a need or I read about someone hurting on social media. When I'm driving, I pray without even thinking about it. When I walk, the same thing happens. We get too religious about prayer. It's a conversation with God.

While it is obviously a serious thing, we don't need to get overly spiritual about it. Just do it. Pray. Be the person of authority the Word says you are. Bind, loose, petition, be anxious for nothing—just pray. This is one of the greatest tools in the hands of every believer. We take it for granted too often. Sometimes that's because we don't see the results we want to see, or at least not in the timeline we would order if we were in charge. But learn to do your part and let God do His part—whatever that might be. It works better that way. Along with that, again, do what the Word says...believe that you receive. How short we often come up on THAT one! We forfeit so many breakthroughs because of a lack of faith. It's commanded of us all through the Old and New Testaments. Listen, he who is strong lives by faith. The weak man lives by sight alone. How are you living?

2. PRIDE VS. HUMILITY. The biggest enemy of going into the Spirit realm with Jesus is that dreaded disease called pride. Conversely, the biggest key I have ever discovered to reaching God is humility. Jesus was lowly of heart. Understand the magnitude of that statement. Jesus, the Son of God, who with the Father created the heavens and the earth and then came to dwell on this sin-filled, fallen planet...was lowly in heart. If He was humble, then so should we be. Regarding pride, I am amazed at what a role it plays in society—ALL parts of society, including the life of a Christian. How will I look if I lose control of my emotions? What will people think of me if I don't remain cool, calm, and collected in a worship service? I could never lie prostrate before the Lord or jump up and down with joy as His presence draws near.

These are all common thoughts for a person who is engulfed in pride. To some degree, I think we all face this stronghold in our lives. I can promise you, in one way or another, it will keep you from God's best in your life. I've certainly had my battles with it, as I told you back in chapter 1 regarding the infilling of the Holy Spirit. There have been many more. That instance is just the tip of the iceberg. Pride got Lucifer kicked out of heaven, and it's been a power tool of his since that day. It can rear its ugly head in any number of ways, often in such a manner that we cannot even identify it—which should speak loudly in itself.

I think this is another reason Jesus often liked being with children more than adults. Much less baggage to deal with, and hardly any pride at all. How refreshing. My Nigerian minister friend and sister in the faith, Elsie Obed, says she doesn't ever want to be an adult Christian when it comes to worship. I like that. She gets that from Matthew 18:3, where Jesus warns us that unless we become like children, we cannot enter the Kingdom of God. Big statement; I'm not sure we really grasp just how big. We all probably need to think on these things more than we do. I agree with Elsie; "Lord make me like a little child in Your presence." When one of my eleven grandchildren hops on my lap to love on Papa for a while, they look into my eyes with innocence and expectation of my expressed love, which is always accompanied by a big hug. Wow.

That's the only example we should need. There's an open invitation from the Father to always spend time with Him, privately and publicly. So just kick pride in the teeth, then let go and let God, as they say.

Humility is the one thing that Jehovah insists on for everyone who lives on this planet. Either we will humble ourselves or He will do the work for us. Rest assured, it's going to happen. I see it every day. I have painful lessons learned the hard way in my own life. I see sports stars with their massive bank accounts and even bigger egos brought down in a hurry when God has had enough. When I think of the verse that says He is opposed to the proud but gives grace to the humble, I always see Him first with His hands straight out in front of Him as to push us away when we're proud. Then I see His arms spread wide with a welcoming "Come here, My child" posture for us when we walk humbly before Him. I always want to be in that second group! The pursuit of humility is a huge downer to all things celebrity.

My former record label president used to jokingly say, "Terry MacAlmon is the greatest worship leader you've never heard of." That statement stung in my flesh but, on the other hand, felt good in my spirit. Trust me, I have fought great battles in an attempt to take the low road—which in God's eye is actually the high road. There are times in the past and still today that I fail miserably. But it remains my goal and quest for life…to be known by God as one with authentic humility…not just perceived humility, but authentic humility. The praise of man is really insignificant to God. Let us all find grace to not want to be seen or acknowledged by anyone but God Himself. I prefer to wait for His reward.

3. SACRIFICIAL GIFTS. In your worship relationship with the Lord, be daring enough to offer Him extravagance from your heart. What's that mean? Well, Mary of Bethany showed us how to do that as she poured a bottle of very expensive perfume on Jesus. Today that might sell for perhaps $20,000-30,000 in the U.S economy. No small act of extravagance there.

When my son Kyle came home from Oral Roberts University to attend my mother's funeral in 2004, he gave me something as we parted that I have cherished from that day until now. He kissed me on my cheek. That may not be such a big deal to you, but it is huge to this father. Kyle had never been one to show great affection or emotion, as it's just not how he is made. Don't get me wrong—his heart is large and very sensitive to the things of the Lord, and he walks a humble walk. Kyle is a modern-day hero, as many years ago he risked his own life to pull three teenagers out of a riptide in Costa Rica. I couldn't be more proud of him, and of all three of my sons. All that said, he's always been on the conservative side of expression. So, when he made the gesture of kissing his dad, knowing this was a difficult time for me and wanting to do something special, he was actually giving me the most extravagant gift of love he possessed. The Spirit revealed that to me a short time later, and I have taught on it many times in the past several years.

Extravagance will mean different things to different people. It may be a large financial offering to God's Kingdom for some of you. Others may want to show their extravagant love by volunteering large amounts of time to a homeless shelter or some other worthy cause. Someone else will spend the night in intercessory worship and prayer. The list goes on and on. What would be your gift that might even end up giving someone or yourself a Whoosh! moment?

4.   **PASSIONATE EXPECTATION.** It's my opinion that the theme of this book—30 Seconds in His Presence—should happen thousands of times in a person's life. I know these experiences are available on a regular basis. I should have had a bajillion more than I have, but life and everything in it get in the way. The more we abandon ourselves to God, the more we will experience the fullness of His Spirit. He wants to be as real to you as He has been to me or anyone else's story in this book. Sometimes we just have to get alone with God and be like Jacob, who said he wouldn't let go until the Lord blessed him. I believe God honors that and will meet us at our point of need, or in this case, our point of desire with Him.

If spiritual genes are passed down through the bloodline, then anything I have of a passionate nature in pursuit of God came from my grandfather. You probably have someone like that in your ancestry too. Audley MacAlmon loved the Lord with everything in him. At one point in his life, this IBM toolmaker decided to hold Sunday afternoon evangelistic meetings in a neighboring town schoolhouse about an hour away from his home in Binghamton, New York. Week after week, he would pack the family of seven into the car and make the drive. My dad told me they would always have to stop and fill the radiator before making the climb up the last big hill going into town. What a visual that is to me. Now for the duration of these meetings, which lasted over a year, there was only one family that ever attended, and they were faithful attenders, but they did not know the Lord. Every week, Grandpa would sing, preach, and then give an invitation to accept Jesus as Savior. And every week no hands would be raised. Finally, my grandpa felt it was time to discontinue the meetings. He announced that he would not be coming up to the little town any longer. Then he preached his final message and gave his final invitation. On this Sunday, every hand in that family went up to receive Jesus. Does this story make you smile? It sure does me. It even makes me tear up a little bit. I wish I had that kind of passionate expectation, not to mention that kind of dedication. And I wish you knew Grandpa Mac. He was quite a guy. His love for the Lord was amazing, complete with LOTS of Whoosh! moments.

5. STAY CONNECTED. Make sure you are attending a church where the Holy Spirit has a chance to move. Friends, we only have one life. Why are we playing games on Sunday with all the religiosity, clock-watching, and the like? We need houses of worship that are drenched with the anointing of God and are offering opportunities for corporate worship to go to the next level. I said way back at the beginning of the book that too many people are going through life without a knowledge of His presence... especially in the "shake and bake" American church these days. Understand that I do get the whole multiple service format. It can't be helped most of the time because of space limitations. But even in that setting there should be an allowance for the Spirit to have a say in things or direct a service down a different path. If your church is stuck in a religious rut, pray for change. God can do anything.

As one of the oddities to the standard institution of the church, I remember watching Robert Schuller's son, also named Robert, conduct a service at the Crystal Cathedral several years ago. He had an unlikely guest, former motorcycle daredevil Evel Knievel. As you may be aware, this is a church that was built around a strict service schedule. Everything ran like clockwork for sure. But...something happened that day that had not happened before, and I would guess not since. Mr. Knievel had recently had a total Whoosh! moment with God, and it changed his life and led him to Jesus. As he boldly and brashly talked about his incredible testimony, complete with quite the colorful language thrown in at unexpected moments, the younger Schuller was moved in a big way, so much so that he cancelled his message and had a water baptism service on the spot for those who wanted to give their hearts to Jesus. How about that!? It was a GREAT moment, televised around the world.

Why and how did this happen? It had to be the fact that Robert had a desire for the real, not just religion. He chose to stay connected and obey the Holy Spirit's voice. If you are a pastor or leader reading this, I have a question for you; what would Jesus say if He attended your church or conference this week? What would He change if His name was on the door of your office? I hope you feel a tad convicted if something comes to mind. We have got to stay connected ourselves so that we can connect people with the presence of the Holy Spirit. He's our best friend. We treat Him as such an outsider or sideline player. He can do so much more than we ever could imagine....and WAY more than our gifts can accomplish.

Along with this thought, make sure you are listening to anointed music in your private worship time. That will give you the greatest boost in getting to a place where you can receive from God. And it will help you stay connected...to Him! Youtube.com has provided an outlet for this. Our own ministry has posted dozens of videos from services, CDs, and DVDs. I know there are hundreds if not thousands that regularly watch as part of their daily or weekly devotion time. If my music doesn't float your boat, I'm sure you can find something else anointed there that will take you to a higher place. God is way cool with technology.

Finally, (there's that word again) I LOVED writing this book! Never thought I would say that. This really was a labor of love, even though the labor did not take all that long to complete, mostly because these things have been in my heart for a long, long time. I pray that each of these chapters has brought you a bit closer to the Lord, helping you to know Him better than when you first cracked the front cover. The Holy Spirit is the real teacher in life. Perhaps He has taught you something you did not know.

If I had to pick just one thing that I hope you will keep in your heart for the rest of time, I would say this again: YOU were made to house the presence of God. It doesn't matter who you are, where you have been, what your history of serving Christ has consisted of, or anything else. You were made for Him. He wants to visit you with Whoosh! moments in every area and season of your life.

As I said before, this book is for you. Please let it be your book. Then add your story to the memory of all these other accounts of His presence. Drop me a line at info@newglory.org and tell me what He has done for you. We're all in this together. The end of time as we know it could be very near. Let's press in to Him as never before. I'm ready for incredible visitations from Him that transform my life and everyone's life around me. It's a new day...time for new grace and new glory.

Yes, Come Holy Spirit!

My Story

Thank you for reading **30 Seconds In His Presence.**

We hope it's been a blessing to your soul!

To order additional copies of this book as well as our music products, or to invite Terry for a Glory Night in your area, please visit our website at

www.newglory.org.

Thank You!

New Glory International

Printed in Great Britain
by Amazon